Security in buildings

General Editor: Colin Bassett BSc, FCIOB, FFB

Cladding of Buildings, *A Brookes*
Electrical Services in Buildings for Architects, Builders and Surveyors, *F. Hall*

Other related titles
Fireplace Design and Construction, *C. Baden-Powell* (George Godwin)
The Refurbishment of Commercial and Industrial Buildings, *P. Marsh*
Joints in Buildings, *B. Martin* (George Godwin)

Security
in buildings
Paul Marsh

Construction Press
London and New York

Construction Press
an imprint of:
Longman Group Limited
Longman House, Burnt Mill, Harlow
Essex CM20 2JE, England
Associated companies throughout the world

*Published in the United States of America
by Longman Inc., New York*

© Construction Press 1985

First published 1985

British Library Cataloguing in Publication Data
Marsh, Paul, 1931–
   Security in buildings.
   1. Buildings—Security measures
   I. Title
   690   TH9705
   ISBN 0-86095-728-4

Library of Congress Cataloging in Publication Data
Marsh, Paul Hugh.
   Security in buildings.

   Bibliography: p.
   Includes index.
   1. Buildings—Security measures. I. Title.
   TH9705.M37 1985   658.4′73   84–29328
   ISBN 0-80095-728-4

Set in 10/12 AM Plantin
Printed in Great Britain by
The Bath Press, Avon

Contents

Preface

Crime has always been a source of concern to large sections of the population; but at no time has this concern been so deeply entrenched and fervently expressed as it is today. On the face of it, it is easy to see the reason. The *Criminal Statistics* have set down their gloomy record, year after year. Successively labelled 'indictable', 'serious' and 'notifiable' offences have risen from half a million per annum in the 1950s, to a million in the mid-1960s and to 2 million in the mid-1970s. In 1981 the total almost reached 3 million.

Security is *the* boom business of the second half of the twentieth century, not only in this country, but in the whole of the Western world. On the one hand, technological development has provided the means to produce ever more sophisticated ways of defeating the criminal and protecting that which does not belong to him from his unwelcome attention; on the other, the very challenge of more defences seems to have generated an eager response in the criminal to outwit the boffins.

Technology today seems to generate action and reaction in direct proportion to its degree of sophistication. We are obsessed by technology. The video boom and the proliferation of home computers is evidence enough of this contention. In the case of more sophisticated security devices, their development has been fuelled by the microprocessor revolution. This year's model is quickly followed by next year's more refined model, reminding one of the heady days of the car boom in the 1960s and early 1970s. This overheated development has encouraged the individual (or organisation) who believes in the motto that 'the latest is the safest' to throw out last year's defences in favour of more technically advanced later models. But is this necessary? And how much safer will premises be? In fact, how worrying really is the increase in crime?

A Home Office Research Study sums up the situation in these words:

> 'Increasingly it is being said that fear of crime in Britain is becoming as great a problem as the crime itself.'

This does not deny the increase in crime, but it does tend to suggest an unhealthy obsession with the subject. Some could say that this quotation represents a whitewashing, an official camouflaging of a truly dangerous situation, and that a preoccupation with crime is justified. This is a subject that will be tackled in Chapter 2 of this book. Against the background of media 'sh ɔck-horror' headlines, the true situation will be evaluated as objectively as possible and vital questions answered, such as how much is it true to infer that there is a breakdown in law and order – and if the situation is honestly deteriorating, in what areas is the deterioration worst and how can this trend be halted, at least as far as the design of buildings is concerned?

We shall take a look at what type of crime is the real threat today – meticulously planned, efficiently executed professional theft, or unplanned opportunist pilfering and mindless property defacement. Also we shall try to make a value judgement on the type of security protection that makes most sense in various types of everyday building. It should be emphasised that this book is about normal buildings – homes, offices, factories, shops and public buildings – not about those specialist buildings with abnormal security problems – banks, security establishments and the like.

Also, because security is a subject which has evoked such an enormous development response today, fuelled by the microchip revolution, it would be impossible for a book like this to remain up to date and relevant if it dealt too closely with the minutiae of the subject. Instead, it is intended to lay the ground rules and indicate the trends which will remain relevant, despite equipment development. It will also enable the specifier to talk knowledgeably with the specialist in whichever sector of the business he is concerned.

No longer are the more complex security systems retrofit items which did not concern the building designer. Today these need to be considered at the design stage, just as are other engineering services, like heating, lighting and air conditioning. As a result the building designer must have a general background to what is going on in the security business, and how relevant the various developments are to the needs of his client. Only in this way can he offer authoritative advice.

Finally the decision as to what level of security to install will have to be taken by the building occupier on the basis of the risk as he sees it, what the equipment will cost and how successful he believes it will be in reducing his risk. It must not be forgotten, however, that the basic design of the building (and the specification of some of its component parts) can have a considerable effect on its security risk level. What is more, in new buildings, this discreet protection need not cost the building owner significantly more money.

To quote the Home Office Research Study once again:

'Criminologists suggest that preoccupation with crime is out of proportion to the risks; that fear is needlessly reducing the quality of people's lives; and that fear of crime can itself lead to crime – by turning cities at night into empty forbidding places.'

Whitewash, or fact? In another part of the Report it points out that

> 'excessive anxiety about crime not only impoverishes people's lives, but also makes it difficult to secure rational discussion of criminal policy'.

This book will endeavour not to add to the public's preoccupation, but it will try to appraise the real risks being run, establish an economic level of protection required in various types of building and, most importantly, look at the way architectural design has in the past helped to bring about the situation in which we find ourselves today and see what it can do in the future to improve what appears to be a very worrying social trend.

Notes

1. Home Office Research Study No. 76: *The British Crime Study:* HMSO 1983.
2. *Criminal Statistics:* England and Wales (Home Office): HMSO (annually).

Chapter 1

What is security?

Many people treat the two words 'security' and 'safety' as applied to buildings as though they were synonymous. This is a serious misunderstanding which needs to be corrected at the outset.

It is true that the dividing line between security and safety is very indistinct and any definition is, of necessity, somewhat arbitrary, but the two subjects are in essence very different and only merge rather confusingly in relation to fire. Therefore it is necessary to set down the definitions which have been used to select the contents of this book.

Safety is taken to mean the protection of the occupants of the building (and to a lesser extent their possessions) from accident; while *security* is assumed to mean protecting from wilful attack those occupants, their possessions and the actual property they occupy. It is really the degree of fortuity which makes the distinction between these two definitions. One is to do with sheer accident; the other with someone's wilful intent. Clearly fire is a borderline case; for while it is usually accidental in origin, and therefore should be considered as being a safety subject, its means of detection and the raising of alarm are so closely linked with parallel security systems that they could not be excluded from this book. Similarly, emergency lighting has been included, because of its borderline nature. Safe evacuation of a building may become necessary because of an accidental happening, or malicious intent. However, fire-protected structures, means of escape and other matters to do with fire, like smoke control and extraction, are considered well beyond the scope of this book and more properly dealt with in a work on safety in buildings.

The subject of security in buildings includes the means and equipment to stop unauthorised entry onto land or into buildings, whether with the intention of committing a further felony or not. Such items as fences and barriers, as well as door- and window-locking systems and security glazing materials fall into this category. Entry systems, which provide selective access to various parts of a building by some people and the exclusion of others, are clearly included, as is the equipment needed to raise the alarm if an intrusion takes place. The special equipment devised to protect valuables or money inside the building from a would-be thief is included, as also is the whole question of vandalism and wilful damage to the building structure and finishes. Most importantly, the way the design of a building can affect its liability to security risk will be considered, along with the way the building itself can impose its own discreet influence on its liability to attack.

What level of security protection?

When we come to consider the type of crime and criminal involved in attacks on people in buildings in the next chapter we shall see that the range of skill and dedication involved is extremely wide. In consequence, the range of security needed in a building will be equally wide, from the very simple security precautions suitable for the average private house, to the extremely sophisticated systems necessary in the large industrial or commercial complex.

The whole subject of security is very much a question of horses for courses. It is as easy to over-estimate the need for security and spend considerably more money than is necessary on sophisticated systems, as it is to under-estimate the risk and lose even more money through burglary. In addition, the security business is a high-pressure, sales-orientated business. The unwary can easily find themselves hustled into over-expenditure on security systems, driven by their fear of an unquantified risk. As a result, in the next chapter we will try to establish the extent of the risk, as far as criminal statistics will allow.

It should always be remembered that advice is obtainable from the local police crime prevention officer. These posts were established in the 1950s, attached to police divisions throughout the country. These officers numbered around 500 by the mid-1970s. Their job is to give a security consultancy service to firms, retailers and the general public in their area. As part of their work they prepare security surveys for commercial and industrial organisations and advise on local crime risks. They are assisted in their activities by Crime Prevention Panels, first established in 1968 and comprising members of local institutions and organisations. These Panels are an attempt to increase community involvement with crime prevention.

The local crime prevention officer would always be able to give objective advice on the level of security required by a particular type of building in a particular area.

Low-level security

This level of security is usually applied to the average protected dwelling and small commercial property. It normally consists of adequate locks on entrance doors, supplemented by mortice bolts, door chains, etc, opening windows with either lockable catches or independent window locks, and possibly some form of one- or two-zone intruder alarm. The latter type is particularly essential in partially occupied premises, or those which combine domestic and sales areas. One zone can protect the unoccupied section of the property at times when the second zone is not activated. Fire alarms are not very frequently fixed in this type of low-security property, although the findings of *The British Crime Survey*[1], which stated that the chances of burglary were slightly less than the chances of a fire in the home, suggest that this economy may be imprudent. Possibly the fixing of some form of independent fire sensor/alarms might be sensible, particularly in split-use property or multi-occupancy buildings. Low-level security is usually adequate for most domestic property and small commercial premises as these (as we shall see in the next chapter) are usually the target of the opportunist, non-professional thief who is easily deterred by minimal precautions.

Medium-level security

This level of protection is usually applicable to the small- to medium-sized industrial and medium-sized commercial building in which at least a proportion of the internal doors are lockable and controlled by a master or grand master key system. The locks are likely to be thief-resistant locks as defined in BS 3621: 1980[2] and distribution of keys will be carefully monitored and controlled. It is possible that there might be some simple form of access control, possibly stand-alone card readers controlling access to certain parts of the site or building. The property would be covered by some form of fire detection and alarm system, even if only manually activated. It is possible that there may be an intruder alarm system which may or may not be linked with the fire alarm system. Depending on the specific nature of the business and its location, there may be other specialist equipment, such as anti-vandal protection in the form of anti-bandit glazing in vulnerable areas (shop display windows, museum showcases, etc.), closed-circuit television surveillance of sales areas or access points and special cash-dispensing equipment.

High-level security

This level of security in the normal type of building being dealt with in this book will be restricted to the largest commercial or industrial complexes. One could expect in these examples a sophisticated and comprehensive access control and recording system, probably integrated into a comprehensive security and management control installation, including fire alarms, public address and energy management – the latter controlling lighting, air conditioning, ventilation and heating control.

This centralised system may well have direct links to the fire brigade and the police and will supply information for a number of management functions, such as personnel absence records and hourly-paid staff wages. The system will most certainly contain highly sensitive automatic activating devices on both intruder and fire alarm systems and it may well make use of closed-circuit television in certain highly sensitive areas.

Types of security protection

Protection of a building, its occupants and its effects fall broadly into four categories:
1. Passive protection.
2. Defensive protection.

3. Fail-safe protection.
4. Specialist devices.

Passive protection

This category has nothing to do with devices or systems imposed on the building, but is to do with the design of the building itself – its layout and its materials of construction. This is the subject largely dealt with in Chapter 3, 'Designing for security'. It concerns the ease with which a building can be attacked, merely by creating in its design areas which are not automatically 'policed' by its own occupants. It also concerns the way the choice of building materials can encourage or discourage vandal attack.

Defensive protection

This form of protection consists of creating a barrier between the would-be assailant and the interior of the building or the site – in other words barrier devices such as locks, access systems, security fencing and barriers. It also includes strengthened portions of the building shell in order to impede illegal entry – such items as anti-bandit glazing etc.

Fail-safe protection

If the barrier devices prove ineffective, this category of protection comes into play. The defences have been, as it were, breached, and the intrusion must be signalled and the alarm raised. As well as intruder detection and alarm devices, this category includes fire detection and alarm systems.

Specialist devices

This category, as its name suggests, includes equipment which is not in general use in most buildings, often to do with cash points or surveillance systems for sales premises. It therefore would contain some special closed-circuit television (cctv) systems, other than normal devices to cover escape doors in sales premises, cash-point security screens and pay counters and even small domestic wall or floor safes.

Some examples of this type of device are included in Chapter 12, although some will automatically be covered in Chapter 9 when pilferage and shoplifting are considered.

Generally the building design has its greatest role to play in the first category of security protection – passive protection. This is more a question of gauging the sociological trends correctly and designing the building accordingly, than in dealing with devices and systems. This, therefore, must be the building designer's greatest concern. Only when all his ingenuity has been exhausted in this respect, should he start to think in terms of defensive and fail-safe protection.

One should always remember that passive protection probably costs the building owner nothing, or next to nothing. The skilful building designer should, therefore, make the most out of this form of security protection, representing, as it does, the best value for money in a highly problematic business.

Notes

1. Home Office Research Study No. 76: *The British Crime Study*; HMSO 1983.
2. BS 3621: 1980; *Specification for Thief Resistant Locks.* British Standards Institution.

Chapter 2

The need for security

Debate over statistics

There can be little doubt that crime seems to be on the increase, not only in Britain, but in the whole of the Western hemisphere. Although this fact is broadly accepted, the extent of the increase is the subject of a fair amount of doubt; the problem arising largely from the way criminal statistics have been collected in the past.

While the amount of crime stayed fairly stable, as it did in the first half of this century in most Western countries, the shortcomings of the statistics were not of major concern. Today, however, when we are facing an apparent fivefold increase in recorded crime since the last war, according to the *Criminal Statistics* based on police returns, we have to be sure that this is the true scale of the increase and not an artificially depressed or inflated one caused by vagaries of reporting crime and recording it.

In England and Wales police and court statistics are published annually under the title *Criminal Statistics*. Police records of what have been called 'indictable' or 'serious' offences, and now are known as 'notifiable' offences are used to compile these statistics – and fairly depressing reading they make. Notifiable offences have risen from half a million in the 1950s to a million in the mid-1960s and 2 million in the mid-1970s. The figure for 1981 was just short of 3 million. Most people tend to accept these figures as representing the *real* level of crime and the *real* rate of increase. But is this true?

Even the compilers of the *Criminal Statistics* warn of the so-called 'dark figure' of unreported crime. The police can only record those crimes which are brought to their notice or which they discover for themselves. It is possible that a substantial amount of crime is never reported to, or discovered by, the police. This is one cause of incomplete statistics. A further complication is the method and care with which the records are made. This has been shown to vary from police force to police force, and from time to time. It was the awareness of the likely misleading nature of the *Criminal Statistics* which has encouraged various countries of the world to start large-scale crime surveys. The United States, Australia, Canada, Israel, the Netherlands and Sweden have all mounted surveys with the intention of discovering more precisely the amount of crime taking place in their countries and establishing rates of increase. In Britain a question on domestic burglary was included in the *General Household Survey*, Office of Population Census and

Surveys, in 1972, 1973, 1979, and 1980, but no extensive crime survey was carried out before 1982, when the first British Crime Survey (BCS) took place.

Overseas experience has demonstrated discrepancies between many crime surveys and the equivalent police statistics. For instance, all seem to prove the existence of a large amount of unrecorded crime, with the proportion of crime recorded by the various police forces varying from one time to another. American crime survey results since 1973 have not, however, matched the increased rate of crime suggested by the police statistics. A similar discrepancy is evident in the Dutch survey results. This could indicate that police methods of recording crime are improving, or they are being more careful to record even the more minor crime. In either case the effect of increased efficiency in compiling the records would produce an apparent inflation of the statistics.

Clearly, the British survey will become more useful as succeeding years' statistics come to hand to be compared. This will allow trends to be established. Nevertheless what it has succeeded in doing so far is to highlight extremely large discrepancies between the *Criminal Statistics* and the BCS interpretation of the facts. It must be remembered that the survey is carried out by interviewing members of the public and asking them if they have been the victim of a crime during the previous 12 months. Clearly this only produces statistics for crimes which have a victim – burglary, assault, theft from the person, wounding, sexual offences, vandalism and the like. So-called victimless crimes, such as shop-lifting and company fraud, are not recorded and therefore we still have little idea of the true extent of the 'dark figure' for this type of crime.

The British Crime Survey

The decision to go ahead with a national survey of crime was taken, as far as England and Wales were concerned, by the Home Office in 1981; shortly afterwards the Scottish Home and Health Department made a similar decision. One person aged 16 or over was interviewed in each of about 11,000 households in England and Wales and 5000 households in Scotland and the findings were statistically extended to draw conclusions for the whole population. Offences were recorded in two main categories: household offences and personal offences. Each offence matched an offence type contained in the *Criminal Statistics*. Table 2.1 sets out the results, as published in the Home Office Study no. 76.[1]

Household offences are expressed as a rate per 10,000 households and personal offences as a rate per 10,000 people aged 16+.

From this it can be seen that recorded crime was a relatively tiny proportion in most crime groups – with the notable exception of car theft where practically 100% of incidents were reported to the police, probably for insurance and repossession reasons. As far as the crimes which related to building design are concerned, twice as many burglaries were indicated by the BCS as were recorded by the police and 13 times as much vandalism. Criminal violence, over which the general built

Table 2.1 Offences in England and Wales in 1981

	Estimated total	Rate per 10k	Percentage recorded
Household offences			
Vandalism	2,650,000	1,494	8
Theft from car etc	1,240,000	700	29
Burglary	726,000	410	48
Theft of car etc	277,000	156	100
Bicycle theft	209,000	118	60
Theft in dwelling	139,000	78	33
Other household theft	1,480,000	835	—
Personal offences			
Common assault	1,490,000	396	—
Theft from the person	422,000	112	8
Wounding	368,000	98	23
Robbery	160,000	42	11
Sexual offences	30,000	16	26
Other personal theft	1,560,000	413	—

Note: Estimated from the British Crime Survey compared to those appearing in the *Criminal Statistics*

environment may have an effect, and including such crimes as sexual offences, robbery and wounding, was indicated as being about five times the recorded level.

These figures appear staggering. For we must not forget that the *Criminal Statistics* themselves have shown a rise of nearly 78% in the 10-year period ending in 1981. However it must equally be borne in mind that the BCS figures were estimates only and did include a high proportion of incidents which were less serious than those recorded by the police. On the other hand the report points out that the survey figures were likely to be underestimates because of respondents' forgetfulness or reluctance to admit incidents. Also the 'dark figure' ratio depends on the type of offence. A very much higher 'dark figure' would emerge if account were taken of offences such as employee theft, shoplifting and many 'victimless' crimes where it is likely that only a very small proportion are reported to the police.

Certainly from questions in the BCS it appeared obvious that for a variety of reasons many crimes were not reported to the police – only one in five cases of vandalism was reported, four in 10 cases of violence (sexual offences, wounding and robbery) and about two-thirds of the cases of burglary. The reasons given for not reporting incidents to the police were mainly that the loss was too trivial, that the police could do nothing, or that it was more appropriate for the victim to deal with the matter himself. It therefore seems likely that the 'dark figure' is not four to five times greater than recorded crime of the *same severity* as it would appear; but nevertheless the 'dark figure' should not be too readily discounted.

Most importantly, the BCS indicates the petty nature of most law-breaking and, at the same time, exposes a huge amount of unreported crime.

The amount of crime

So what does all this mean to the public at large? What scale of risk does the average person or his property run? Only when this is established can an assessment be made of the real need for security. Also only when the type of criminal likely to be involved is known can a true assessment be made of the right form the security should take.

It is very easy to express criminal statistics in over-emotive ways, guaranteed to throw the public into varying degrees of panic – and these are often the tactics employed by some of the less scrupulous high-pressure salesmen in the security business. It is quite alarming to be told that of the crimes classified in the BCS, one incident is happening throughout the country every three seconds, and roughly one household burglary is happening every minute. But these same statistics can be looked at differently. For instance, if the total number of offences in the BCS were shared out equally between all the police in England and Wales, each officer would have to deal with one offence every four days. Alternatively, the average home can expect to be burgled once every 40 years – and this is a high rate when compared with the average person of 16+ years suffering robbery once every five centuries, assault resulting in injury once every century and have his family car stolen once every 60 years. These figures are of course worked out on the basis of the 1981 crime figures applying throughout the periods specified – a highly unlikely state of affairs.

But before we feel too comforted by this way of looking at the level of crime, we should remember that different types of people suffer different risk levels. Also differently located property suffers greater risks of being burgled; for instance a house in an inner city might be burgled on average once every 13 years. The average person generally can expect to be the victim of a burglary or car theft once or twice during adult life. The chances of being injured in an assault are very much smaller, and the risks of robbery are smaller still. More trivial offences, such as vandalism or minor theft, could be expected by the average person once every three years.

It is interesting to compare UK crime figures with those of other countries. The incidence of burglary in this country is slightly higher than the rate in the Netherlands, roughly equal to that in Australia, lower than in the seven main Canadian cities and half the rate in the United States. The UK rate of car theft is comparable with that in Australia, but higher than in the Netherlands, the United States and Canada. Robbery is more frequent in the United States and Canada; while our levels of vandalism are roughly mirrored in the Netherlands.

Opportunist crime

Because of the generally trivial nature of the vast majority of crime, it seems likely that its occurrence is very much influenced by the availability of a suitable opportunity. The BCS did note that 'huge amounts of property are left with minimal security in houses, offices, shops, and on the street' and indicated that much crime resulted from carelessness on the part of the victim.

Home Office Research Study No 34; *Crime as Opportunity*[2] examined this premise against the background of two surveys – one looking at the effect that the fitting of steering column locks has had on car theft, the other examining the effects of supervision on buses on the incidence of wilful damage. The report concluded that the most expedient form of crime prevention was to remove the opportunity to commit an offence; i.e. making the crime more difficult to commit. This, the report believed, would discourage the opportunist offender and deter the professional by increasing his chances of being apprehended. Physical crime prevention, it stated, would probably prove more cost-effective than trying to change would-be offender's attitudes. It also made the point that the design of buildings had a major part to play on the incidence of crime – a point that will be taken up in the next chapter.

The report did note that there was a tendency once one opportunity was removed to displace the crime to another victim area. For instance, when in 1971 car manufacturers started fixing steering column locks, there was a tendency for car theft to be concentrated on older cars without column locks; and when supervision was placed on buses, vandalism which had been experienced on the top deck was displaced to less visible areas depending on the position of the stairs.

En passant, the report noted the conditions likely to encourage theft. Firstly there had to be a ready supply of stealable goods (precisely the conditions created by the self-service shop as opposed to the old-fashioned corner shop); secondly there had to be a demand for those goods; and finally the careless attitudes of the public to the protection of its goods positively encouraged theft. There are a few additional points which should not be overlooked. In most types of property these days there can usually be found a quantity of relatively easily removable, high price equipment (minicomputers, videos, television sets, stereos, electric typewriters), all of which are in high demand and readily saleable. Also, with the general availability of personal transport, easy getaway is assured and the area of operations of the thief can become extremely large. Finally, disappointing though it may be, there seems today to be less public stigma attached to some forms of crime, reflecting a general decline in public moral standards.

The inference to be drawn from this Home Office Study is that the majority of crime is undertaken by small-time or non-professional criminals (often teenagers) looking for an opportunity to make a quick killing. They are not the well-organised professional thieves, who often work in groups, carefully plan their operations and are seeking substantial rewards. Such criminals would be more likely to concentrate on buildings with an abnormally high security risk – buildings which are outside the scope of this book.

So as a general rule, normal building security is primarily concerned with defeating the opportunist thief or the mindless vandal. The well-planned, professional break-in is relatively rare in normal buildings unless the rewards are attractive enough. The only exception to this is possibly the large commercial firm with valuable commercial secrets to be stolen – the type which is likely to be equipped with the most sophisticated security system, which we shall be examining later in this book.

10

also a possibility with so many computers.

Burglary

Burglary is one of the most popular crimes (with the possible exception of shoplifting, of which we have few reliable statistics). According to the *Criminal Statistics*, the most frequently committed crime is theft and handling stolen goods (approximately half the total in 1981), followed by burglary (approximately one-third of the total). Only 29% of residential burglaries were 'cleared up' during that year, compared with 41% for all serious offences.

Legally speaking, the act of burglary is committed when someone enters a building as a trespasser and commits – or intends to commit – theft, criminal damage, rape or wounding. Forced entry is no longer a criterion of burglary, although it is often a characteristic of the crime. Impersonation of a workman or meter reader in order to gain access to a property is considered burglary.

The BCS put the burglary rate at 410 per 10,000 households (including attempted burglaries). This figure does not take account of burglaries not involving dwellings. In only a fifth of the cases where burglars actually entered the home was insurance compensation paid out, indicating partly the large number of properties which are not insured and partly the low level of loss involved in the burglary. Table 2.2 shows the value of theft losses recorded in the BCS. Set alongside these figures are others derived from another Home Office research carried out in 1979 on samples of property in three areas of Kent (Home Office Research Study No 74; *Residential Burglary*[3]). It will be seen that these two sets of figures do not match up. Similar discrepancies will be noted later between these two surveys' findings. This only serves to indicate how sparse our definitive knowledge of the whole business of crime, and burglary in particular, really is.

The BCS went on to note other characteristics of burglary that its researchers uncovered. Like the Kent Survey, it noted that it is highly unusual for the burglar deliberately to vandalise or soil the premises he enters, in spite of a common belief to the contrary. It also seems extremely unlikely that a violent confrontation would take place between the burglar and the householder. The BCS noted that the risks of burglary in inner city locations are double those in other areas of conurbation and five times those elsewhere. Flats are more likely to be burgled than houses (although

Table 2.2 Value of theft losses in burglaries

Value	BCS percentage	Kent sample (1979) (%)	Rest of England and Wales (1979) (%)
Attempt only	39	14	20
Nil or under £5.00	16		
£5 to £99	22	55	69
£100 to £499	13		
£500 +	9	31	11

Note: Expressed as a percentage of total incidents: BCS statistics compared to Kent survey and general 1979 statistics.

this might merely be because flats tend to be in cities) and houses at the end of terraces are more likely to be burgled than centre terrace houses. It did not find any other significant differences in risk between other house types. This is not borne out by the Kent survey, or by the General Household Survey of 1979/80[4] as is shown in Table 2.3. The BCS did, however, note a higher risk in rented, than in privately owned property – a characteristic noted by other researchers.

Finally the BCS noted that homes left unoccupied for several hours a day were more at risk than those which are more or less permanently occupied. This agrees with the Kent survey, which further pointed out that most burglaries (when the approximate time of entry was known) took place during daytime (between 6.00 am and 6.00 pm). Only 7% of a general sample of houses surveyed presented the burglar with any real problem; i.e. had security installed to the crime prevention officer's recommendations. Table 2.4 shows the level of security found in the survey sample.

Table 2.3 Influence of building type on risk of burglary

Type of dwelling	Kent survey: % of victim sample	General Household Survey incidents per 1000 dwellings
Detached house	50	25
Semi or small terrace	31	22
Bungalow	16	—
Long terrace	1	27
Others	1	purpose-built flats: 38 converted flats: 47 flats with businesses: 78

Note: Derived from the Kent study and the General Household Survey 1979/80

Table 2.4 Sample of household security

Security level	Households (percentage)
Good security	
Burglar alarm	3
Good door-locks and locks on all windows	2
Good door-locks and window-locks on downstairs	2
Partial security	
Some doors without good locks/some downstairs windows without locks	66
Poor security	
No good door-locks or window-locks	28

Note: Levels of domestic security discovered in a general household sample examined during the Kent survey

Twenty-two per cent of the break-ins occurred through an insecure door or window in the survey of the Kent burglaries. The favourite point of entry seemed to be a rear window, followed somewhat distantly by a rear door and a side window. It also seemed that most burglars are quite prepared to break glass to get at the window catch or door nightlatch. The chief items stolen were jewellery or cash, followed by electronic equipment.

The Kent survey made some very interesting comments on the influence that the surroundings of the property can have on the burglar's decision whether to attack a property or not. These will be taken up in detail in the next chapter. Seclusion certainly seemed to be a valuable asset for the burglar and a rear garden which was not overlooked by neighbouring property and in which he could go to work at leisure seemed to be a major criterion of property selection. A ready escape route was also an important feature. This survey, unlike others, tended to suggest that the relative levels of security did not play too great a part in the burglar's choice of target. This came fourth behind lack of occupation, seclusion (which it calls a property's *environmental risk*) and reward (i.e. the value of the haul). In other words, top on the burglar's hit list would be a large, high rateable value house in its own grounds, in the country, distant from most other houses, not easily visible from public areas and frequently left unoccupied. This would be closely followed by a high rateable value house, in town, also frequently left unoccupied, usually with a fairly large garden which screened it from the road. Even a busy road, in these circumstances, would not put the burglar off.

In assessing the risk to a property, according to the Kent survey, it seems that the four attractions to the burglar are low occupancy (often left empty), high reward (easily disposable goods – high value, low bulk), high environmental risk (not overlooked etc.) and, finally, poor security. It will be argued later that the low priority set on security is not justified.

From Table 2.3 it will be seen that property which combines living and shop accommodation is particularly at risk, according to the General Household Survey. This should always be protected by some form of two-zone intruder detection/alarm system. Lock-up shops, particularly if the goods for sale are easily disposable and high value (jewellers, electronic goods shops, alcohol and tobacco sales premises), are also very much at risk.

The BCS points out that the majority of burglaries are committed by teenagers who are highly apprehensive about encountering the householder. They want to take a small amount of goods quickly. Many are totally unskilled in their art and will act on impulse if presented with an opportunity, but will equally well give up if the property appears reasonably secure and move on to one that is less secure. As this is typical of the vast majority of properties, they are not lost for choice.

The higher current rates of burglary, particularly teenage burglary, could well be encouraged by high levels of unemployment. Not only is this stealing for gain, but also stealing from sheer boredom and even as a misplaced protest against a society which is not providing enough jobs.

In many cases of both residential and commercial burglary a little bit of foresight on the part of the occupants could have probably saved considerable loss. Often the burglar entering an office is only looking for the petty cash box, which more often than not he will find at the back of a bottom or middle drawer in a filing cabinet, the keys for which he discovers (where he expects to) in a desk drawer. A little originality in hiding places and greater care of keys might have been sufficient protection.

Shoplifting

In 1983 a report by the Home Office Standing Committee on Crime Prevention, *Shoplifting, and Thefts by Shop Staff*[5], noted the continuing rise in the rate of theft from shops. In 1981 there were 225,342 offences of shoplifting recorded by the police; clearly a figure that in no way represented the complete scale of the problem which cost the British shopkeeper an estimated £1,000 million per annum, although the clear-up rate of 89% was quite high. The figure for such offences in 1969 was 91,169; in 1982 more than 242,300.

The report, however, indicated that this disturbing trend was more the result of opportunist crime than the work of professional criminals, although it did point to a worrying incidence of gang theft in some cities, involving groups up to 50 strong, and intimidation of the shop staff. It also indicated that the way shops are organised today does tend to make pilfering more easy.

Various methods of improving security were suggested, most of which had to do with the training of the staff, but some involved the layout of the stores; and these points will be dealt with in the chapter dealing with pilferage and shoplifting.

Vandalism

This is a particularly mindless crime in that, apart from the vicarious thrill the vandal may receive from actually breaking objects or defacing surroundings, there is no benefit to the perpetrator. It is defined as the intentional and malicious damage to property and is equated with the category 'criminal damage' in the *Criminal Statistics*. As far as the BCS was concerned it included arson, damage to the home and damage to motor vehicles. It excluded the much greater area of vandalism aimed at shops, schools, telephone kiosks and the like. Nevertheless, even with these major exclusions, the survey yielded a staggering amount of vandalism at a rate of 1500 incidents per 10,000 households, 13 times as much as was included in the *Criminal Statistics*. Slightly more than half those cases uncovered by the BCS involved motor vehicles, and therefore had little to do with building security, except that the majority of these cases occurred to cars which were regularly parked in the street, possibly belonging to households without garages. The risk of vandalism increased with urbanisation, but not apparently to the extent noted in the case of other offences.

It is interesting to note that in the Manchester area over 90% of the local authority spending on vandalism is directed towards council house and school repairs. In the

3-month period from the beginning of February to the end of April 1978, 1052 repair documents were issued in respect of schools and 1968 in respect of housing, giving a total expenditure of £153,020. During the same period, 7552 cases of wilful damage were recorded by the Post Office in telephone kiosks. Meanwhile, also in the same period, the Greater Manchester and Merseyside police recorded 6603 criminal damage offences.

The problem is huge. Its increase seems roughly to reflect the breakdown of parental and teacher control, and a decline in society's respect for property. Chief offenders seem to be pre-teenage and teenage boys who, acting in a group, appear to equate acts of vandalism with proof of manhood.

Research was carried out in 1978 to see if television advertising could be used in one area of the country to change children's and parents' attitudes to vandalism. The experiment is reported in Home Office Research Study No 63: *Crime Publicity: an Assessment*[6]. This report makes depressing reading. The effect of the advertising campaign proved to be negligible. However, in contrast, there appeared to be success in the case of another campaign; this one mounted by the Devon and Cornwall Constabulary in 1975. This urged parents and teachers to warn children of the installation of intruder alarms in a number of schools. Clearly the suggestion was that the odds against intruders being caught had dramatically shortened, and children involved with break-ins in order to commit acts of vandalism were not slow to grasp the implication. In this case at least, the hardware of security was seen to pay off as a deterrent.

Summary

As explained in the preface, it is not the purpose of this book to increase the preoccupation of the public with crime – a preoccupation that is seen by some as being unhealthy. However, the facts contained in this chapter must leave no doubt that, although the extent of the crime explosion may not be so huge and so violent in content as it is sometimes painted, there does exist a very real problem; and one that faces every property owner – the problem of how to protect himself, his possessions and his property from illegal attack. The risks of such attack certainly are increasing and, as far as one can see, will continue to increase. No one seems to have found a way of changing the attitudes of the potential criminals to criminal activity and until this happens an apparent slip into lawlessness, in minor crimes at least, would seem to be inevitable.

Looking at the problem from another point of view, it would seem impossible for any police force to cope with the considerable increase in minor crime which we are experiencing today. They have enough difficulty coping with the major criminals who are learning to fight sophisticated security systems with ever greater sophistication. It is also arguable whether the police should be seen as the major deterrent of the majority of minor crime. The responsibility may best be placed on the public to protect itself by using appropriate security methods.

Society will have to find its own long-term solutions to the apparent slip into lawlessness. It is not enough to blame underemployment – a situation which seems likely to remain with us as technology replaces people with microchips. Society will have to take a new look at moral standards and respect for property, coupled with a more responsible attitude towards the training of the young. But this will be a slow programme of regeneration. In the meantime it is up to every property owner to look after his own property.

In spite of the findings of the Kent burglary survey, in which security was placed relatively low on the deterrent list, other surveys have suggested that pretty basic precautions can deter many criminals. It could be that in the Kent example there was a larger proportion of 'professionals' at work than may be found in other areas of Britain, further away from London and less well known as areas of affluence. And of course it must not be overlooked that all these burglaries had in fact been reported to the police, and therefore did not form part of the 'dark figure' as did many of the examples discovered in the BCS. So it must be concluded that the property owner would be unwise not to pay great attention to rendering his property secure. Nevertheless, bearing in mind the large degree of opportunist theft, unless his possessions are extremely attractive to the professional thief, very basic security precautions are often good enough.

All surveys remark on the apparent carelessness of the average householder in locking up his property, particularly during the daytime when his home at least is at greatest risk. As the Home Office Research Study No 74 put it: 'At its lowest level, then, sensible security should simply include closing windows and locking doors, particularly when the house is left empty'. But locking the door and closing the window is only worthwhile if the design of the door and window matches the sturdiness of the lock. This is a subject that will be dealt with later in this book.

Although personal violence is the type of crime that appears to worry most people, there is little evidence that the risks from it are increasing at a rate comparable with the increase in vandalism and burglary. The public's fear of burglary is often coloured by fear of a violent confrontation with the intruder. This rarely occurs. What is more, the wanton destruction and soiling of the home by the burglar is equally rare. So the conclusion to be drawn from all this is not one which should increase the public's anxiety and obsession with crime, but merely increase awareness of the need for the building owner or occupier to take proper precautions to protect his property and its contents. These precautions should be in proportion to the risk that his property runs, its type, location and the value of its contents. It is not a problem warranting panic, but one that merely needs a little bit of objective thought.

The need for security? Yes; but *reasonable* security.

Notes

1. Home Office Research Study No. 76; *The British Crime Survey*; HMSO 1983.
2. Home Office Research Study No. 34; *Crime as Opportunity*; HMSO 1975.

3. Home Office Research Study No. 74; *Residential Burglary*; HMSO 1982.
4. General Household Survey 1979/80; Central Statistical Office; HMSO 1983.
5. Home Office Standing Committee on Crime Prevention; *Shoplifting, and Thefts by Shop Staff*, HMSO 1983.
6. Home Office Research Study No 63; *Crime Prevention Publicity: an Assessment*; HMSO 1980.

Chapter 3

Designing for security?

Many thousands of words have been written and spoken on the subject of the quality, or lack of quality, of the built environment we have created through the last 40 years or so. Generally these words have taken the form of a lamentation in which it almost seems that the whole blame for all our present social ills can be laid at the door of contemporary buildings – their design and the way they relate, one to the other. This is a bitter judgement and one that is clearly a somewhat simplistic generalisation. Nevertheless, one is bound to admit that many of the new building forms which emerged in the years of rebuilding after the Second World War did little to cure our social ills and may, quite often, have exacerbated some of society's problems, all of which have their root in human weakness.

One only has to look at high-rise flats to understand this accusation. There is no doubt that this form of accommodation was downright unsuitable for many who were put to live in it; and yet at the time these blocks were designed, the architects were pursuing a logical and understandable sociological theory. They argued that with rocketing land prices, maintaining a need for high-density housing, coupled with the need to rehouse displaced inhabitants of demolished slums, where densities were usually so high that their reproduction was undesirable, it was preferable to form high-density living zones by piling accommodation units one on top of the other, rather than create a similar density in a wider urban sprawl. The high-rise blocks at least gave the opportunity to surround the blocks by park land – amenity areas for all to enjoy.

The problem was that the architects and planners were being too naive and were forgetting that society is made up of a percentage of villains who can turn any idealism into nightmare. And so not only were the high-rise blocks anathema to the young wife with small children, who could not supervise their play except within the safety of the flat; and disliked by the old who were afraid of the lifts and public circulation areas and felt lonely and out of touch with life around them; but the open spaces soon became ill-kempt and shabby and the scene for many unsavoury activities which had never entered the heads of the architects who designed them.

In a sentence, much of the building design since the war has lacked realism and a proper understanding of the character of the people who make up society. What is more, we still have not purged ourselves of this shortcoming, in spite of finally deciding to throw out high-rise flats. Milton Keynes, the low-rise new city, has been designed with spacious open areas and cultivated infill spaces between the developments – areas which are extremely expensive to maintain, are already starting to look tatty and are impossible to police. The winding pedestrian ways, removed from the dangerous proximity with traffic routes, have developed their own form of danger, becoming fertile locations for the less desirable activities of the socially malevolent.

Sad to say, idealism in the design of the built environment only works with a society made up entirely of socially biddable people. Such a society has never existed and probably never will. It is therefore the obligation of architects and planners to curb their idealism and design realistically to ensure secure living, working and recreation opportunities for the inhabitants.

What is secure design?

Designing with security in mind is not merely a matter of remembering to include in the specification of the building such items as will prevent unwanted access – door and window locks, shutters and fences or access control systems; nor is it merely a matter of designing into the building methods of giving early warning of attempted illegal entry or the outbreak of fire. Important as both these aspects are, they are the more obvious methods of providing security for a building's occupants and their possessions and will be dealt with at length in later chapters. Here we are looking at the less obvious ways the design of a building and its relationship with other buildings will enhance or diminish its chances of attack.

We have seen in the previous chapter that a large proportion of crime is of an opportunist nature. What we are trying to analyse here is what creates that opportunity – apart from obvious failings like leaving an external door wide open? In his book, *Defensible Space*[1], Oscar Newman uses the following words:

'Crime rate may not correlate specifically with density, but it *does* correlate with building height and type. Unfortunately, above eighty units per acres, there appears to be only one building prototype available – the high-rise, double-loaded corridor, elevator tower – and that option does correlate strongly with crime rate.'

Newman arrives at this conclusion from an extensive study of North American housing developments and the incidence of crime in and around them. He arrives at eight ingredients for a high crime rate related to public housing projects. They are:

1. A project housing over 1000 families.
2. A project containing high-rise blocks over 7 storeys high.
3. An area surrounding these blocks which is not penetrated by city traffic.
4. Grounds around the development which are designed as one continuous space, not as a series of plots related to individual blocks.
5. Each block housing between 150 and 500 families.
6. Blocks designed around one central lobby.

7. Blocks having corridor access to flats which are situated on both sides of the corridor (double-loaded corridor).
8. Blocks with lifts positioned centrally and escape stairs positioned away from the lifts.

To illustrate the influence of height on the incidence of crime, Newman quotes the statistics shown in Table 3.1 based on New York City Housing Authority Police statistics for 1969. Here the felony rate in the 3-storey building is 9 per 1000 population, as compared with 20 per 1000 in the case of the 13-storey or over blocks. What is more, the crime rate in interior public spaces (corridors, lifts, stairs and lobbies) in the higher blocks adds up to a massive 54.8% of the total number of crimes, as opposed to 17.2% in the case of the lower blocks. From this it seems that the larger and more inhuman the building, the more prone it is to crime, which ranges from petty vandalism, through drug abuse, to assault and theft. It is interesting to note that crime taking place in the interior of the flats or in the grounds of the buildings are considerably higher percentages of the lower crime rate in the low-rise buildings. This suggests that the rabbit warren layout of larger buildings with greater lengths of corridors and more stairwells, encourages the activities of the criminally inclined.

Generally the conclusions that Newman formulated were that fear of apprehension was the major deterrent to the would-be criminal, and his unease would be increased if he believed (a) he might be recognised as an 'incomer' by the residents of the block, and (b) he did not have a ready means of escape if his presence were challenged. Hence, the larger the block, the less likely is it that the residents will recognise an intruder and the less inclined they become to challenge anyone's right to be in the building. In fact the larger the block, the less proprietorial interest the tenants seem to take in it. They tend not to identify with it and even their

Table 3.1 Locations of crime in different sizes of apartment block

Location of crime	3 storey building (mean felony rate 9 per 1000 popul.)	13 storey + building (mean felony rate 20 per 1000 popul.)
Grounds	42.4%	23.8%
Apartment interiors	40.4%	21.3%
All interior public spaces	17.2%	54.8%
Subdivided into:		
lobbies	7.2%	8.1%
halls	3.3%	10.8%
elevators	1.3%	22.6%
roofs	1.3%	4.0%
stairs	1.3%	5.9%
social spaces	2.8%	3.4%

Note: Statistics relating to the location of crime in two sizes of apartment block, compiled by the New York City Housing Authority Police and quoted in *Defensible space* by Oscar Newman particular part of the block does not seem to have that same sense of 'ownership' attaching to it as, for instance, to the terrace houses it replaced. In addition, the escape stairs which the fire regulations demand give a ready means of escape to the criminal and one which tends, by its very use, to be enclosed in solid walls and therefore poorly supervised. Such conditions make the policing of the block impossible and, even if an alarm is raised quickly, escape for the criminal is practically assured.

In fact the policing at all times of all areas of any development, whether residential or commercial, is impossible and therefore the imposition of normally accepted standards of behaviour is brought about more by the combined disapproval of the majority than by professional policing. But for society to be generally self-policing, the individual members of society have to feel a proprietorial interest in the area in question, they have to know who should be there and whose presence should be questioned and they have to be able to see and be seen from the public areas surrounding their ownership.

This is at the heart of the theory of defensible space expounded by Oscar Newman. He defined it in residential terms as an 'environment which can be employed by inhabitants for the enhancement of their lives, while providing security for their families, neighbours and friends.' He also set down four conditions for a secure environment as:

1. Territorial definition of space in which areas inhabited by the occupier, whether inside the building or outside, clearly belong to the occupier and are seen to belong to him.
2. There should be natural surveillance of exterior or interior public space from the inside of the building.
3. The building form should not advertise the isolation of its occupants.
4. The siting of the building should not be adjacent to activities which could provide a threat.

Although Newman was developing his theories against a residential background, they equally hold good for other locations where normal day-to-day social activities take place.

Jane Jacobs in her book, *Death and Life of Great American Cities*[2], points out that streets with pedestrian and vehicle movement are more secure than empty streets and emphasises the danger inherent in desolate no-man's lands left between pockets of differing development. These 'border vacuums', as she calls them, are commonly produced in our cities today as a result of development of one sort or another. New urban motorways are particularly guilty of the creation of this form of derelict land. Milton Keynes is full of examples and will probably remain so for a long time to come – maybe forever.

In reality the planning ideal of open space is hardly feasible if the public is afraid to use it – a not unusual situation. Public parks should be easily supervised from surrounding roads and open space round housing developments should be overlooked by the windows of the surrounding property. One of the recent planning fashions – the Radburn layout – deliberately turned all the major windows of its houses away from the public areas surrounding them so that each property overlooked its own private garden.

From the above a few general principles of design emerge which, if borne in mind, should help to reduce the likelihood of crime, not by locks and fences, but by a series of tacit manipulations of space.

Obvious ownership

The design should help to emphasise the ownership of the building and the space around it. There are innumerable historic precedents for this from the basement area in front of a Georgian terrace house to the canopy, spacious approach steps and surrounding flower boxes of an office entrance. Not only does this warn off the intruder by giving a clear indication of ownership, it also reinforces the owner's sense of property. As we shall see in the next chapter which deals specifically with vandalism, there is nothing so encouraging to the criminal as an apparent no-man's land. Equally, there is nothing so demoralising to the occupier if the land outside his door carries no sort of indication that it is within his area of influence.

In a recent study carried out on 18 housing estates in Lambeth by a team from the Shankland Cox architectural practice, the report recommended that the space round buildings should be divided into three zones: recognisable private space (possibly gardens), semi-private space (maybe a courtyard shared by 20 to 50 dwellings and forming an area within which an intruder would be noticed), and a public zone beyond the shared area.

Surveillance

All public areas immediately surrounding a building should be overlooked by that building's windows. This is particularly important at access points, which ideally should be overlooked by more than one property. This presents a difficulty in that it would appear in some respects to diminish the occupier's privacy, and a balance needs to be struck between the needs of security and the desire for privacy.

Surveillance is particularly important in the case of internal public spaces. These must not give the impression of safety to the would-be criminal. Lift lobbies should not be tucked away out of sight but preferably should be capable of being seen from the entrance.

Clearly in multi-occupancy buildings it is ideal if there is some form of access control, either mechanical, or in the form of a doorman. While this is quite possible in commercial buildings and expensive apartment blocks, it is not possible in low-cost housing.

The GLC has noted that the shape of its school buildings affects their security. Concealed internal courts which are screened from sight from the school keeper's house are areas which are particularly vulnerable.

22

Building size

Particularly in the case of residential buildings, it is desirable to keep the number of units per entrance down to a size at which strangers using the entrance become obvious. It is always a good idea to try to group units in such a way that a group identity develops. In this way there is more chance of a pride being taken in the building, and the public areas will be cleaned and looked after.

Escape routes

In spite of the difficulties which undoubtedly will be encountered, escape routes should lead to a position which can be supervised and not just discharge, as is so often the case, onto open ground at the back of the building. Stair wells should be given as many observation panels as possible, positioned so that landings can be seen by casual passers-by. This will clearly be limited by the needs of fire protection. It has been suggested that in order to avoid escaping criminals switching their routes, escape stair doors should not permit access from the stair onto intermediate floors, only at ground level. In other words, once having entered the stair, one can only leave the stair at the escape level. This system does, however, have drawbacks.

Open space

This should be identified with the buildings within the space and should be overlooked by their windows. It should be linked to the pedestrian and vehicle routes of the city so that passers-by act as a deterrent to intending wrong-doers.

Lighting

All public areas within or outside the building should be adequately lit naturally or artificially so as to avoid patches of deep shadow. Luminaires clearly will have to be of a vandalproof type.

To sum up; the planner and building designer must, during the whole design process (but particularly during the earliest formative sketch designs), consider the security of the development's occupants and their property. In addition to supplying the building with the necessary devices to avoid burglary etc., the designer should plan his building to make it uncomfortable for the criminal to operate. This will not deter the professional thief with a firm intention to attack a particular property, but it will do much to deter the opportunist criminal who contributes so much to present-day crime statistics. In addition, it certainly will have a significant effect on the level of vandalism (to be discussed in the next chapter), which does much to demoralise an area and start an inexorable slide into more serious forms of crime.

Notes

1. Newman, Oscar; *Defensible Space*; Architectural Press, 1972.
2. Jacobs, Jane; *The Death and Life of Great American Cities – the Failure of Town Planning*; Jonathan Cape, 1962.

Chapter 4

Avoidance of vandalism

According to the Criminal Damage Act 1971, a person is guilty of an act of vandalism if he or she 'without lawful excuse destroys or damages any property belonging to another intending to destroy or damage any such property or being reckless as to whether such property would be destroyed or damaged'. In other words, vandalism concerns the wilful damage of property, whether or not this property is perceived as belonging to anyone or not, resulting in remedial action having to be taken by someone other than the person effecting the damage.

Generally the crime of vandalism is a very safe and anonymous offence, rarely leading to the perpetrator being apprehended, and from which he or she receives no reward, except possibly a vicarious thrill from the act of destruction. The majority of examples are carried out by children and are the result of the more anti-social and uncurbed aspects of play. Later this originally unintentional vandalism can develop malicious overtones, followed sometimes in later life by 'instrumental vandalism' – wilful damage which is not an end in itself, but is an adjunct to another crime, such as theft from a telephone box. There is also a comparatively small number of incidents which have other motives, such as revenge against an individual or institution, frustration with authority, or even acts which have a political motive. These are usually committed by older persons.

In 1978 the number of cases of criminal damage in England and Wales reached 300,000, but many crimes are not reported and do not get added to the criminal statistics. What is more, Home Office statistics only record cases of malicious damage in which the cost is over £20. It has been estimated that the total annual cost of vandalism in England and Wales is at least £100 million. Schools come in for a substantial share of the abuse. One typical industrial city with a population of 500,000 has reported around 4000 cases of vandalism a year, of which 2500 occurred in schools. Of its total bill of £150,000, £61,000 went on repairing damage in schools and £44,000 on repair to houses.

The Consortium for Method Building, a group of seven local authorities, including some rural counties such as Somerset and Berkshire, estimates that wilful damage to public buildings costs its members around £200,000 a year.

Unexpectedly, the problem is not confined to inner city areas. Of the 398 schools in Berkshire, 269 were reported to have suffered from vandalism in one year, at a total cost of £122,400.

So it can be seen that the problem is by no means a small one; a fact of which most people will already have become well aware if ever they have searched for an unvandalised telephone box. But the cost of vandalism cannot be measured alone in expenditure on repair or reinstatement. The harm goes much deeper than that and includes distress to those who live surrounded by the effects of vandalism and a general demoralisation which creeps into such areas and which seems to encourage further vandalism.

Why vandalism?

The causes of vandalism are extremely complex. Often architects become the whipping boys for society's ills. The whole burden of guilt for the lack of pride in the built environment, which results in vandalism, is heaped on their shoulders. While design has to bear a share of the guilt, it alone did not cause vandalism, nor can design of supreme excellence eradicate vandalism.

The majority of vandalism is committed by the young – often by the very young. The density of the children in an area is a critical factor in this particular social problem. A survey of London housing carried out by Sheena Wilson, when she was at the Home Office Research Unit, discovered that all types of buildings where the ratio of school-age children was above 5 to every 10 dwellings were likely to be vandalised. The same applied to blocks which boasted a total number of 20 such children. High-rise blocks, which house large numbers of children, were particularly susceptible to vandalism. The habit of vandalism therefore seems to grow up within a pack of children when they are allowed to play, unsupervised, and where the less desirable elements of their play are allowed to develop unchecked.

Vandalism is very much an opportunist crime; and therefore flourishes in situations where the scale and anonymity of the surroundings induce a lack of sense of ownership and belonging in the inhabitants – in fact, the type of inhumanity discussed in the last chapter.

Vandalism case study

To illustrate the complex mixture of ingredients which encourages vandalism, the case of the Cunningham Road scheme, initiated by the National Association for the Care and Resettlement of Offenders (NACRO) and carried out jointly by Social and Community Planning Research (SCPR) and NACRO, is worth studying in some detail.

Cunningham Road is a council housing estate of Halton District Council in Widnes which in the mid 1970s was drab, uncared for and subject to considerable vandalism. It had a population of approximately 1600, of which nearly half were under 17 years old. The houses were mostly two storey with front and rear gardens; 250 dated from around 1950, while 200 new houses and flats had recently been completed when the scheme commenced at the end of 1975. An effort was made to improve the situation, based on the assumption that if people could be encouraged to like the place they lived in and feel a sense of ownership, they would look after it. The strategy involved finding out the views of the tenants and making improvements based on these views.

A full summary of the scheme and its findings, written by Ann Blaber (former Crime Prevention Officer for NACRO), is included in The Design Council book, *Designing against Vandalism*[1]. In this the author sums up the original situation in these words:

'When we started, the older part of the estate was run down: a few houses were boarded up; others, though occupied, had broken windows. Most of the gardens were untended; fencing was a jumble of corrugated iron, wire and old boarding. The shops were barricaded with steel shutters, and daubed with graffiti. The streets were in poor condition, the pavements worse, and there were no trees in public places. Some of the houses are of concrete block construction, and were grey and streaked by nearly 30 years of pollution. There were signs of vandalism all over the old part of the estate: broken glass, graffiti on 'undefended' walls, smashed brickwork, and litter strewn around gardens, pavements and streets. The new part of the estate with its timber-clad and brick terraced houses and open-plan frontages looked much more attractive, but even there the playgrounds had been vandalised and the paving was littered with glass.'

This is hardly encouraging material with which to start. Ann Blaber's account tells how a method of consultation was set up with the tenants. From this it seemed that their main anxieties were about security and dissatisfaction with the council's performance over repairs and maintenance. The young complained of having nowhere to go and nothing to do; the older people were troubled by the disturbance and destruction caused by the young people.

Many of the maintenance problems were brought about by poor detail design in the older properties; also the fencing policy in both new and older parts of the estate had been unsatisfactory – open frontages in the newer part, and a lack of authority-provided fences in the older part. The newer houses had exacerbated dissatisfaction with the older properties. The whole scenario was one that was clearly angled at disillusion and demoralisation.

The methods employed to tackle the problem did not, in fact, cost the council an enormous sum. The fence problem was tackled with the intention of reinstating in the tenants a pride in ownership. Tenants were encouraged to plant their own hedges. A more regular maintenance and repair discipline was introduced. This seems to be a vital factor in the avoidance of vandalism. Broken windows are a direct incitement to vandals – and many broken windows were caused merely because of the poor design of the windows in the older properties. Also tenants were allowed to choose the colours their houses should be painted. Pavements and street lighting were repaired and, at the tenants' request, a beat policeman was assigned to the estate.

As far as the young people were concerned, an adventure playground, started before the scheme began, was opened and a playleader was appointed who involved mothers with playground activities and organised children to plant trees and start a mural on one of the walkways.

After 2 years, the scheme could not be said to be an unqualified success, but the estate is considerably improved. The adventure playground had a faltering start, being completely vandalised within weeks of its opening. After being closed for a while, it reopened and has been operating successfully since. Generally the estate is more tidy; there is less broken glass and litter, empty houses do not need to be boarded up and most of the newly planted trees are still standing. Vandalism and crime have not disappeared, but whereas a few years ago no one would have dared to stop teenagers causing a disturbance or breaking things up, now the public seems more inclined to make their feelings known. Much of this seems to have resulted from the tenants now having a greater pride in the place they live and being more involved with their neighbours.

From this example it can be seen that the control of vandalism is as much a matter of sensitive social management as anything to do with the environment and the buildings. Nevertheless, the built environment does have a contribution to make.

Effects on vandalism of design

Design can have considerable influence on the likelihood and severity of wilful damage. There are four ways in which a designer can discourage vandalism or minimise its effects. They are:

1. Building and neighbourhood design can help to generate a respect for the area in its occupants, as well as a sense of belonging. People generally appear to respect attractive and well-maintained environments – particularly those which reflect a human scale and which create a community feeling. People find it difficult to identify with large-scale, inhuman developments. These, coupled with an impersonal 'authority' which does not seem to care about individuals' problems, create a recipe for disaster.

    One way of inducing a sense of belonging in housing developments is to arrange the areas of land surrounding the properties so that they identifiably belong to those properties and the people living in them. This aspect has already been covered in the previous chapter. Not only does this enhance pride of ownership, it also discourages vandal attack. Vandals rarely attack property which appears to belong to an individual. The only exception, of course, is vandalism resulting from a revenge attack.

2. The design of the built environment must help a society to police itself. Developments which turn their backs toward the public areas are more prone to vandalism than those whose windows overlook such areas. Surveillance, as we discovered in the previous chapter, is an important deterrent to all forms of crime – vandalism no less than burglary. As we have seen, vandalism is a very anonymous crime and flourishes on anonymity. The shyness of the vandal is well illustrated by the dramatic increase we have seen in graffiti since the introduction of the readily-concealed aerosol can. A bucket of whitewash and a brush were rather more obvious burdens and their very explicitness made graffiti a less attractive method of expressing frustration.

3. The designer does have an obligation to use components in his design which are man enough for the job. This is not always an invariable habit, largely due to a failure to visualise the level of normal abuse to which everyday items are put, or simply to a lack of sufficient funds. But any economy made in this area is thoroughly mistaken and is a long-term waste of resources. This approach is not based on the assumption that every item has to be made abnormally strong, but merely *strong enough*. The GLC, among many other authorities, has discovered that building failures are one of the commonest triggers of vandalism. What is more, neglect is infectious and broken windows beget more broken windows. Also equipment containing items of value should be deliberately designed to make them difficult to get at to avoid instrumental vandalism. Good examples of this are bank cash dispensers which are practically never attacked, as compared with the much-vandalised telephone boxes. Particular examples of vandal-prone items will be examined in a later section of this chapter.

4. Finally the designer should take steps to ensure that the consequences of vandalism do not cause unnecessary damage. For instance, it is always advisable when designing a school or public toilet to ensure adequate floor drainage so that, if a flush cistern is broken, the water flow does not damage surrounding areas. In other words, the designer should always maintain a realistic view of the likelihood of vandalism and make provision in his design if the worst does happen.

Building components and materials chiefly at risk

The Building Research Establishment published a Digest (No 132) which set out to study wilful damage on housing estates[2]. It arrived at a number of design recommendations – mostly things to avoid if later vandalism was to be discouraged. These included such things as: soft textured and easily damaged wall surfaces, or walls in public areas of light colour; glass in vulnerable positions and breakable plastic covers to low-level light fittings; plastics or asbestos-cement fall pipes within 2 m from the ground; lead and copper external pipework and soft mortar joints; easy access to flat roofs, tile hanging and non-robust up-and-over doors with handles at knee-height (vulnerable to kicking); lever handles on all types of building except those occupied by the old and infirm; painted metal posts and rails in play areas; excessive amounts of soft landscaping; cobbles and setts which can be used as missiles; and easy-to-climb ranch board fencing and thin overhanging copings on low walls. It also made a general recommendation concerning the avoidance of dark corners in entrance halls and similar unsupervised locations – the creation of what the GLC has christened 'vandal temptation zones'.

This Digest broadly covers the major problem areas, but it may pay to examine some special types of buildings a little more closely.

School vandalism

Schools, because of the relationship between the young and vandalism, become the focal point of much wilful damage. The degree of vandalism seems to correlate closely with the type of area in which the school is situated. Generally urban schools are more heavily vandalised than rural schools, and urban schools in areas of poor quality housing are considerably more prone to vandalism than all other types.

One of the difficulties is to recognise the difference between accidental and wilful damage. Many areas of school building come in for considerable rough usage, which is not intended to cause damage; and it must be remembered that we have already established that damage begets further damage, and something that starts out as an accident can cause an epidemic of vandalism. For instance, once the children realise how to gain access to the inside of a convector heater, they will want to do it again and again.

Less supervised areas such as changing rooms and toilets appear to be the major vandal temptation zones. Clearly toilet cubicles have to be chosen with care, firstly to be strong enough and secondly not to arouse the climbing or swinging instincts of the children. Sanitary fittings should be strong and pipework and flush cisterns as far as possible concealed. Also wall surfaces should be such that they either discourage the graffiti artist or are easily cleanable. All these remarks apply equally to public toilets. The GLC has decided that the layout with toilets scattered around the school at convenient points for the pupils is maybe, in terms of wilful damage, a wrong approach. Such areas tend to become indefensible areas that seem to belong to no one. Therefore it is tending now to plan central toilet blocks which can be supervised, maybe by the person responsible for cleaning them.

Doors and windows in schools tend to be frequently damaged, both wilfully and accidentally. Schools suffer many break-ins. This alone is sufficient cause for strong door and window frames and locks, and the use of anti-vandal glass or polycarbonate in vulnerable areas. The subject of security glass will be dealt with in the next chapter.

Fire raising is one of the most serious forms of vandalism and this seems to have concentrated in recent years on school buildings. Between 1969 and 1974 the number of school fires almost trebled – a situation which was exacerbated by the use of new materials with a low resistance to fire. This should be borne in mind by the school designer. Some authorities have considered it wise to install fire detection equipment and some now have a policy, particularly in the case of isolated schools, of installing intruder alarm systems. Much protection can be given to schools in populated locations by designing the buildings so that they are overlooked by neighbouring properties.

Vandalism in shopping areas

Protection of commercial premises is more a question of protection against theft than vandalism, although vandals each year cause a considerable cost to shopkeepers in broken windows. In some cases special vandal-resistant glazing may be advisable. This subject is dealt with in detail in the next chapter.

The rears of lock-up shop premises are particularly vulnerable to vandalism and attempted break-ins. Here it might be sensible to use window grilles or other similar protection and the door should be very strong and fitted with thief-proof locks (see Chapter 5).

Many of the peripherals of shopping areas are more subject to vandalism than the shops themselves. Multi-storey car parks and staircases, subways, passages and lifts leading from the car parking space to the shopping area are good examples of indefensible space and therefore at risk. If these areas cannot be 'designed out' of the scheme, the following thoughts should be borne in mind. Surfaces should discourage graffiti. Tough glazed ceramic tiles, for instance, are recommended, although expensive when compared with untreated concrete. Mechanical equipment, such as lifts, should be of the robust vandal-proof type. Also good lighting is essential in these areas, although light fittings are common targets for vandalism.

Lighting equipment should be robustly constructed. Such items as transparent lanterns in all but the most remote locations should be made of unbreakable polycarbonate rather than glass; low-level fittings should be vandal-resistant bulkhead units which make forced entry extremely difficult; and doors to control gear compartments in lighting columns should be unobtrusive and difficult to force.

Another important aspect of lighting in these types of area concerns its maintenance. Lighting should be regularly and systematically checked and repaired. Neglected damage (or even normal usage wear) will quickly encourage malicious damage.

Vandalism on housing sites

This subject has already been discussed at length in this chapter and the materials particularly at risk have been summarised in the BRE Digest No 132. However, once more the peripherals need further mention.

Garage areas are typical vandal temptation zones. They should be overlooked by the surrounding properties and not tucked away where no one can see them. Individual garages should not be provided with windows. Even if they are too small to climb through, they can make the damaging of cars inside possible. Climbing on garage roofs is a common occupation and one that can prove quite dangerous if the old asbestos cement sheets have become brittle. As a result the roofs should be protected by wide overhangs and easy methods of climbing on to them should be eliminated. The doors to the garages, too, should be strong enough to resist a fair amount of attack.

Vandalism to street furniture

One group of items of street furniture – exterior light fittings – has been dealt with earlier. Most items, like seats, litter bins, planters, etc. attract the attention of vandals and should be strong, made of non-corrodible materials and have surfaces which are not easy to deface. In addition they should be firmly anchored in position and all fixings should be concealed.

Notes

1. Design Council: *Designing against Vandalism*, The Design Council, 1979.
2. BRE Digest No 132: *Wilful Damage on Housing Estates*, Building Research Establishment.

Chapter 5

Avoidance of intrusion

Apart from prohibiting unwanted access to the environs of the building by means of security fences, barriers and gates – a family of devices discussed in detail in Chapter 11, *External security and security lighting* – the prevention of intruder access into a building is usually based simply on locking its points of entry (windows or doors) and reinforcing those areas of evident weakness in the building shell (such as window glazing). This physical exclusion of unwanted access (*defensive protection* as defined in Chapter 1) is often backed up by *fail-safe* protection, in the form of intruder alarm systems which are triggered by a forced entry or an attempt at a forced entry.

Locking systems may be controlled in a variety of sophisticated ways, which will be examined in more detail in the next chapter where the subject of access control is discussed. Here, however, we shall take a look at straightforward locks and locking systems, security glazing and intruder detection and alarm. There will follow a short section on other security devices associated with doors and windows.

Locking systems

Locks fall broadly into two mechanism categories; those with lever mechanisms (in this category can be included the Chubb security locks which replace levers with detainers) and those of a cylinder type. This latter type can be subdivided further into those with pin tumbler and those with disk tumbler mechanisms.

All locks have one or more square-ended bolts, which are shot into a hole in the locking plate (or box soldered to the locking plate) by the operation of a key. It is this which distinguishes locks from the manually operated bolts on doors and windows. The lock is fitted to the opening component (door or window), the locking plate to the frame.

Most locks are operable from both sides of the door, except those developed for doors intended for single-sided entry (prison cell doors and some cupboard doors). Exceptions to this are some cylinder locks which are operated on one side (usually the outside) by a key and by thumb turn on the other side.

Latches are devices which have a bevelled springbolt or roller bolt. These latch automatically on the closing of the door, the bolt being withdrawn by the action of the door handle or, in the case of cylinder nightlatches, by the operation of the thumb turn on one side and a key on the other.

Locks and latches are either mortice pattern, in which case they are morticed (or let into) the thickness of the door at its meeting edge and held in place by screws through their forends, or rim pattern (i.e. fixed to the inner surface of the door by screws).

Lever locks

The levers in a lock are a series of flat movable detainers which have to be moved by the action of the key to lock or unlock the door. The bellies of the levers in a lock are cut away to various depths to provide different combinations (i.e. to provide the lock with a degree of individuality which makes it only openable by its own key). The notches (or bitting) in the end of a key blade are formed to operate the levers, making the key special to a particular lock (Fig. 5.1).

There are various numbers of levers in a lock, but most of the security locks from well-known manufacturers have five levers. BS 3621: 1980[1] insists that a thief-resistant lock should have at least five levers. It further requires any lock having eight levers (Fig. 5.2) or less to include some form of anti-pick device such as false notching. The more levers, the greater is the degree of individuality of the key and the more scope for providing lock differs. Many lever locks also have wards. These are fixed obstructions inside the lock case which preclude the wrong key being moved into the correct position to operate the levers. The blade of the key is notched on its side faces to pass over the wards as it is moved into position below the levers. The use of wards increases the number of differs that can be obtained in a lock. Some low-security locks make use of wards only. These are not to be recommended as wards alone give little security. Warded locks can be turned using a skeleton key, but skeleton keys cannot be made for lever and cylinder locks.

Cylinder locks

Cylinder locks and latches, as their name suggests, contain a cylinder which houses the pin or disc tumblers and springs. These have to be moved by the key to operate the lock (Fig. 5.3). The mechanism of a pin tumbler cylinder is as follows. The cylinder contains a coaxial plug. This is restrained from turning by a number of pin/driver combinations which are forced into drillings in the plug by springs in the body of the cylinder. The pin is the leading section of the combination; the driver the following section. When the right key is inserted it forces the pins back against the springs until the joint between the pins and drivers line up with the intersection between the plug and the cylinder, thus allowing the plug to be rotated and the lock operated. It is the teeth-like notchings (or bitting) in the upper edge of the key which operate the pins and drivers.

Cylinder locks offer very high security against key interchangeability and anti-pick mushroom drivers are included in the best cylinder locks. These are drivers

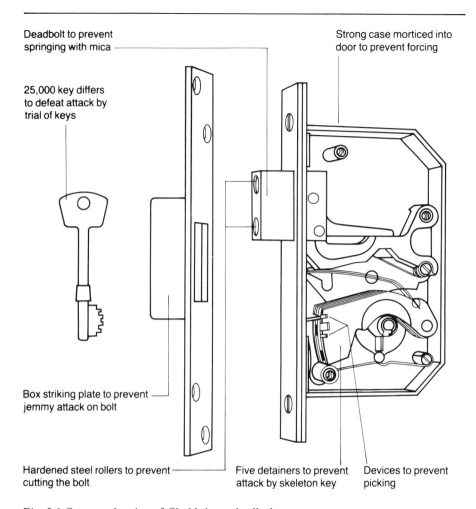

Deadbolt to prevent springing with mica

Strong case morticed into door to prevent forcing

25,000 key differs to defeat attack by trial of keys

Box striking plate to prevent jemmy attack on bolt

Hardened steel rollers to prevent cutting the bolt

Five detainers to prevent attack by skeleton key

Devices to prevent picking

Fig. 5.1 Cutaway drawing of Chubb lever deadlock

which are tapered and have a mushroom-shaped head. They cannot be lifted by a lock-pick. When manipulated they tilt and wedge. BS 3621 insists that a thief-resistant cylinder lock should have at least four anti-pick drivers out of the minimum of six driver/pin combinations required of a security lock (Fig. 5.4). Clearly, as with levers, the greater the number of pins, the more special the key needed to operate the lock and the greater the number of differs possible. Five-pin cylinders can offer up to 24,000 differs with ease and they are very suitable for master keying and suiting.

Cylinder locks with disc tumblers operate in much the same way except that small shaped discs are substituted for the pins.

There are a number of special forms of cylinder lock on the market which are operated by keys which look dissimilar to the conventional cylinder lock key, notably the Kaba-20 security cylinder and the Abloy system. The former is based

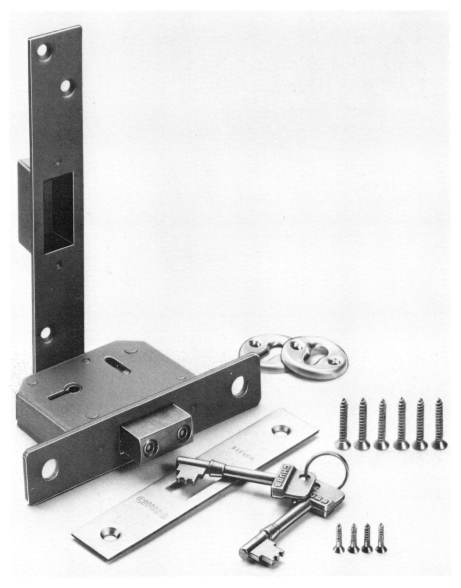

Fig. 5.2 Chubb Economy mortice 5 lever deadlock

on a pin tumbler system; the latter on a disc tumbler system. In principle, however, the methods of operation of the locks are similar, but the uniqueness and the availability of the key blanks to make replacements or duplicates often sets these locks apart from all but the most highly secure of the conventional lock ranges.

In addition there are a number of electric locks which contain an electric motor which can override the mechanical unlocking of the door with a conventional key.

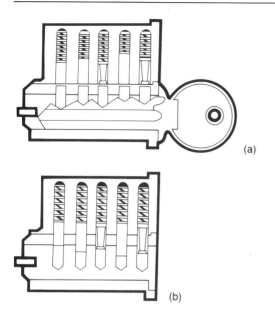

Fig. 5.3 Diagram of a cylinder lock (a) with and (b) without the key in position

Fig. 5.4 Kenrick Unilock Range

There is also a group of locks, used especially on access doors where maximum security is necessary, which have electric strikers which can be released from remote security locations. Both these types of lock can be used in conjunction with access control systems and will be dealt with in more detail in Chapter 6.

Vulnerability of locks

Locks can be vulnerable to illegal entry by two major methods: forcible attack, and lack of key security.

Forcible attack

Locks can be subjected to attempts to break the lock by forcing. This is usually defeated in security locks by ensuring that the lock is stronger than any wooden door into which it is fixed. In other words, the door breaks before the lock.

A jemmy attack on the lock bolt can usually be defeated if the bolt shoots into a steel box, soldered to the locking plate (see Fig. 5.2). This protects the head of the bolt from prizing by a jemmy. Additional protection from jemmy attack is provided by those locks, such as the Era Invincible lever lock from J. E. Reynolds and Co., which when locked have the bolt, bolt stump and levers in line. This offers a particularly strong resistance to jemmying.

The cutting of the bolt through the gap between the door and frame can be defeated if the bolt contains hardened steel rollers. These reinforce the strength of the bolt and, if an attempt is made to saw through the bolt, they will merely rotate with the action of the hacksaw blade. Such rollers can be seen in the bolt shown on Fig. 5.2.

Some cylinder nightlatch bolts can be slid back using a sheet of mica or plastic (see Fig. 5.5). This is only possible if the locking snib has not been set to deadlock the bolt. This cannot be done, of course, from outside. The result is that the premises are most vulnerable to this form of attack when they are unoccupied – just the time when the greatest security is needed. A more secure form of nightlatch is one that double locks. A simple opposite turn of the key in the outside cylinder deadlocks both bolt and inside knob simultaneously. This gives protection, too, against the breaking of a wood panel adjacent to the lock in order to operate the snib.

Most security locks contain anti-pick devices (false notching in the case of lever locks and mushroom drivers in the case of cylinder locks). Skeleton keys will not operate on lever and cylinder lock mechanisms. (Note: warded locks can be vulnerable to skeleton key operation.)

BS 3621 requires that all fixings of thief-resistant locks should be inaccessible when the door is locked, that the vulnerable parts of the lock should be protected from drilling by anti-drilling plates and that if there is a handle on either one or both sides of the door, its breaking will not release the bolt. It also requires the throw of the bolt to be at least 14 mm measured from the forend of the lock.

Fig. 5.5 Attempting to slide back the bolt of a nightlatch type of lock

Key security
The better ranges of security locks are noted for their number of levers or tumblers. The more of these, the more differs of lock are possible and therefore the less likely it is that a key not made for a specific lock can be found to fit it.

Some manufacturers, such as J. Legge and Co., produce 5-lever locks to BS 3621 which have been designed to replace existing 2- or 3-lever locks, requiring a minimum of work on the doors and their existing mortising.

Also the better security lock keys are difficult, if not impossible, to make to fit a series of locks.

Most suppliers of security locks have a special procedure for ordering additional keys for high security locks and for master and grand master keys (see later). This involves the registering of the key or suite owner, whose signed authorisation is required before additional keys will be supplied. In some cases this authorisation has to be countersigned by someone who has to approve the issue of all keys, even to approved key owners.

The highest degree of key security occurs when a cylinder lock is subject to control by *one key only*. Any security lock purchased from one of the larger manufacturers from their standard range of differs will provide considerable key security. BS 3621 recommends that any thief-resistant lock should provide a minimum of 1000 effective differs and we have already seen that a Yale 5-pin cylinder lock offers up to 24,000 differs as standard. However, to provide maximum security, Yale introduced in 1964 a range of *high-security differs* which provide a one key operable cylinder mortice deadlock and a high security padlock. These are produced from special 6-pin blanks which are not available to the trade. Additional keys are obtainable only from Yale. With each lock a registration card is provided to enable the purchaser to enter thereon his name, address and specimen signature of the only person authorised to order additional keys. This card is returned to Yale.

BS 3621 insists that the lock manufacturer shall maintain differing charts of his standard ranges of security locks so that BSI inspectors can verify that the locks have been manufactured in such a way that no lock having the same differ as any other lock is made until at least 999 other locks, each effectively differing from all the others, have been made.

In buildings with a considerable number of locks it is clearly inconvenient to have all the locks differing and requiring separate keys. This is particularly important in the case of the need for emergency access to all parts of the building. Two alternatives are available. All the locks can be of the same differ; i.e. one pass key will operate all the locks; or a master key system can be introduced. The advantage of master key systems is that it does not allow general access to the whole of the building by every key-holder. Only a master key-holder has such a facility.

Master keying

A simple master key system is an arrangement whereby a number of locks can be operated by a master key, although each lock is also operable by its own individual *change (or servant) key* (Fig. 5.6). Sometimes it is convenient to arrange for a set of locks within the suite *to pass* (or *alike change*); i.e. all the locks in the pass group are of the same differ and can all be operated by the same key (pass key) as well as the master key. Such a group is known as a pass group.

40

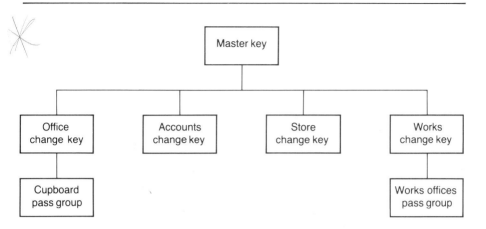

Fig. 5.6 Diagram showing the suiting arrangements of a master key system

In larger buildings it may be desirable to divide the premises into a series of distinct areas within which total freedom of access is required for certain responsible individuals, but whose freedom of access should not extend to other sections of the building. Then it is necessary to introduce a *grand master keyed suite* (Fig. 5.7). This is an arrangement whereby a series of sub-suites are introduced, one for each area of the building. Each suite is controlled by its own master key (known as a sub-master key), while the grand master key opens every door in every suite. In particularly complex buildings it may be necessary to introduce a sub-grand master into the hierarchy, controlling two or more sub-suites, but not all of them.

A specialist version of this type of suiting of locks is the case of an apartment block or hotel in which all the entrance doors to the flats or bedrooms have different locks, yet each change key can be used to operate one or more common entrance doors. In this case master keys can be supplied, if specified, to all locks, including the entrance door locks. It must be borne in mind, however, that in a suiting such as this (often referred to as an apartment suite) where so many different keys operate the entrance door lock, this lock cannot be regarded as a security lock.

Ordering locks

The basic information required by the lock manufacturer when ordering locks is as follows:
- type of lock
- quantity
- size (if applicable)
- finish
- whether to differ or be alike
- quantity of keys per lock, and
- the 'hand' of the lock, if applicable.

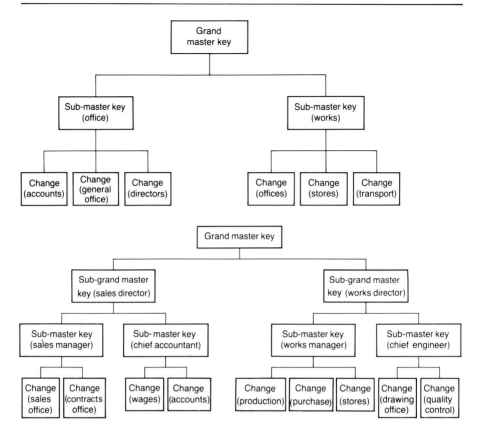

Fig. 5.7 Diagram showing the suiting arrangements of a grand master system

It is necessary to state the hand of a lock when ordering mortice nightlatches, mortice two-bolt locks, rebated locks and latches and cupboard locks. Whether a lock is left- or right-handed is decided by imagining yourself standing outside the door, facing the door. The side on which the lock occurs, as you see it, whether the door is inward or outward opening, is the hand of the door (Fig. 5.8). The ISO method of handing doors refers to clockwise closing (CC) and anti-clockwise closing (ACC) in conjunction with either the opening face (OF) or closing face (CF). CC-OF and CC-CF doors are right-handed; ACC-OF and ACC-CF doors are left-handed.

Other information will be required in the case of some locks. For instance, an outward opening rim nightlatch will require a reverse bolt and striking plate. This should be specified. In the case of a rebated mortice lock (used on double doors), the size of the mortice should be given. Also detailed information will be required if master or grand master key systems are needed. The manufacturer should be consulted at an early stage.

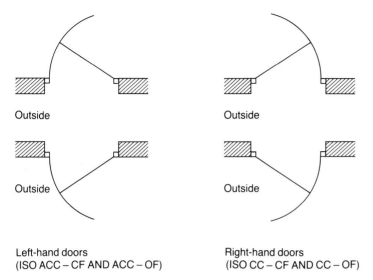

Left-hand doors
(ISO ACC – CF AND ACC – OF)

Right-hand doors
(ISO CC – CF AND CC – OF)

Fig. 5.8 How the handing of a door lock is determined

Note: In considering locks it must never be forgotten that any lock is only as secure as the door to which it is fixed. If the door or its frame can be easily forced, there is little point in using an expensive security lock. This is particularly true of doors with thin wood panels or adjacent glazing. Also the fixing of the lock must be correct, using the fixing devices supplied by the lock manufacturer.

Security glazing

Normal annealed glass is an extremely fragile building material, providing little or no protection against forced entry or vandal attack (see Fig. 5.9). Also, it is easy to cut relatively small holes in a sheet of glass, holes large enough to insert a hand and manipulate a thumb turn of a nightlatch or raise a casement catch, without making much noise. This needs to be borne in mind when specifying door and window furniture.

Glass is also quite a dangerous material. One safety expert has been quoted as saying: 'If someone tried to introduce ordinary glass onto the market today he would certainly be prevented from doing so by existing safety regulations'. In fact up to 40,000 people in the UK every year suffer from accidents involving glass in buildings. And this danger has been recognised by BS 6262; *Code of Practice, Glazing for Buildings*[2]. This highlights areas of particular danger and stipulates that in these areas some form of safety glazing should be used. It should be emphasised, however, this is all to do with *safety*, not *security*. And some forms of safety glazing materials are very little defence against a thief or vandal.

Three classifications of impact-resistant glass or glazing plastics were laid down in BS 6262. These materials to gain a classification had to pass various stages of an

Fig. 5.9 Steel ball falling onto ordinary annealed glass (photograph courtesy of Monsanto)

impact test set out in BS 6206[3] (based on the American Z97 test). The grades range from Class A, the toughest grade, to Class C, the lowest grade of safety glazing recommended.

One of the important things to appreciate about the BS 6206 test is that the glazing is deemed to have passed the test if the glazing has not broken, or if it has broken safely; i.e. not like ordinary annealed glass, in a series of sharp, dagger-like pieces. This allows toughened or tempered glass to pass the test. This is annealed glass which has been heat treated. It has about five times the strength of ordinary annealed glass, but when broken shatters completely and safely into a multitude of tiny fragments. A non-laminated car windscreen is a good example of this. This makes toughened glass hardly an adequate deterrent to a burglar or vandal.

Wired glass, on the other hand, is annealed glass in which has been embedded wire reinforcement. When the glass shatters, the pieces are held together by the wire, still forming a barrier to the intruder. The same applies to laminated glass. This is normal glass bonded to one or more inner layers of plastic, usually polyvinyl butyral (PVB) (Fig. 5.10). This holds the glass together when it breaks. It is said to be impossible to cut a hole in laminated glass without access to both sides of the glass. The strength of laminated glass depends on the number and thicknesses of the plies. For instance, the Impactex range of laminated glass from Alcan Safety Glass covers a range of strengths from Class C safety glass (2 layers of float glass, 1 layer of PVB and a thickness of 5.4 mm) to bullet-resistant glass with a considerable number of plies and a thickness of 50 mm.

Fig. 5.10 Steel ball falling on Monsanto laminated glass. The glass remains adhered to the Saflex interlayer

Clearly for normal anti-intruder protection, the use of a quite simple laminated glass would prove sufficient deterrent. There are, however, two special types of security glazing materials for particularly hazardous locations. These are each covered by a British Standard. Anti-bandit glass is covered by BS 5544: 1978[4] and bullet-resistant glass by BS 5051; Part 2; 1976[5].

Anti-bandit glazing material is supposed to be able to withstand severe attack by such weapons as bricks, hammers, crowbars or pickaxes. It will also provide considerable blast protection (as well as not permitting the bomb to be thrown in through the window). This type of glazing is intended for vandal-prone locations or places where the snatch thief might operate; shops, banks, post offices, museums and kiosks.

Bullet-resistant glazing, according to the standard, comes in five qualities, G0, G1, G2, G3 and S. The G classifications will withstand various forms of handgun or rifle; the S classification a shotgun (see Table 5.1). These glazing materials are clearly used in high-security areas where attack by firearms is a distinct possibility.

Polycarbonate glazing material is good for anti-bandit purposes where high surface quality and the durability of glazing are not of primary importance. In composite form, polycarbonate bullet-resistant panels can be manufactured.

As with all glazing, it is important that the actual process of fixing the glazing should be carried out correctly. There must be no risk of water lodging at the edge of the laminate as this could ultimately be absorbed and cause delamination. Efficient,

Table 5.1 Impactex Bullet-resistant glasses

BS 5051 classification	Details of weapon: type, calibre etc	striking velocity	Details of ammunition: type	mass	Range	Number of strikes*	Thickness of Impactex required to satisfy Standard
G0	Handgun, 9 mm military parabellum; 254 mm barrel	405 m/s ±15	9 mm MkZ2 Standard	7.5 g	3 m	3	26 mm RS, 30 mm RS, 26 mm†, 30 mm†
G1	Handgun, 0.357 magnum; 222 mm barrel	450 m/s ±12	Soft point, flat-nose bullet	10.2 g	3 m	3	35 mm RS, 35 mm†
G2	Handgun, 0.44 magnum; 222 mm barrel	471 m/s ±9	Soft point, flat nose bullet	15.6 g	3 m	3	40 mm RS, 40 mm†
G3	Rifle, 7.62 mm; 533 mm barrel	830 m/s ±9	7.62 mm ball Nato standard	9.5 g	10 m	3	50 mm RS, 50 mm†
S	Shotgun, 12 bore magnum (full choke); 711 mm barrel	360 m/s ±30	76 mm magnum cartridge, BB shot	46 g	3 m	2	35 mm RS, 35 mm†

*Pattern of strikes: for classifications G0, G1, G2 and G3, equilateral triangle, strikes 100 mm apart within a 200 × 200 mm square in centre of sample; classification S, two shots coincidental in centre of sample.

†To conform to BS 5051 these glasses must be fitted with a secondary splinter screen.

self-draining gaskets or non-shrink compounds and sealants should be used and the glazing material should be given the correct bedding and edge-coverage around its entire perimeter. Special anti-bandit and bullet-resistant glass may need special consideration and the manufacturer's advice should be sought.

Finally there are on the market a number of security films that can be adhered to normal glazing in order to upgrade their strength. Many of these are quite capable of upgrading ordinary annealed glass to the level of a safety glass and some can provide considerable protection to occupants of a building from flying glass in the event of the detonation of a bomb.

Specifying security glazing

When specifying security glazing it is important to establish precisely what are the risks that the glazing is likely to run and choose a glazing material which provides the right degree of protection. Over-specification can be a very expensive business; under-specification can, in extreme cases, prove very costly in life, as well as in property. Make sure that the performance of the material specified has been authenticated by independent test.

Intruder detection and alarm

Intruder alarm systems vary from quite simple, domestic scale systems, to extremely complex components of an integrated security system, including fire protection, access control and even the energy management of the building. These integrated systems will be considered in detail in Chapter 10.

Simple intruder alarm systems consist of three elements: the detection device, the control unit and the alerting device.

Detection devices

These devices can range from simple magnetic contacts set in the reveals of windows or doors to sophisticated movement detectors which sense the environmental changes brought about by the presence of an intruder, or react to an obstruction in a radiated beam. Broadly detectors fall into two categories: *passive* detectors and *active* detectors. The former category contains microswitches or magnetic switches on doors or windows, pressure pads, vibration and acoustic detectors – all detectors which operate as the result of a signal generated by the intruder; the latter category contains those detectors that generate their own signal which they radiate into the protected area. These are sometimes referred to as volumetric devices when they fill an area with radiation, as opposed to radiating a beam directed towards a receiver. While the conditions remain the same in the protected area, no alarm takes place, but when movement occurs, altering the pattern of the reflected radiation (or the breaking of a beam of radiation in the non-volumetric types), the alarm is activated. These detectors include ultrasonic, microwave and infra-red detectors. Passive detectors tend to react to attacks on the building fabric, the forcing of an entry or the unwarranted movement of doors or windows; active detectors react to movement within the building. To these two automatic sources of alarm should be added those devices which can be deliberately activated by the occupants of the building – personal attack buttons etc.

Building shell attack detectors

The magnetic contact fitted to the opening edges of doors and windows is the simplest form of these devices. They are referred to as *protective switches* in BS 4737[6]). Once the system is set, the opening of any protected window or door will trigger off the alarm sounder by breaking (or closing) an electrical circuit. Access by the owner of the property without setting off the alarm is usually permitted by means of a special pass lock, often situated on the frame close to the main lock on the access door. This deactivates the system. Alternatively a mortice deadlock with a microswitch connection, known as a shunt lock, can give the same facility without the need for a special key.

The glass in the windows can be protected by a variety of means. The traditional method is a non-adhesive or self-adhesive metallic foil, secured to the glass (a *foil-on-glass detector* according to BS 4737). This will generate an alarm condition if the window glass is broken. Other methods include a vibration detector fixed to the glass (particularly used on large glass panes such as shop windows) or a small acoustic detector fixed to the glass which responds only to the sound of breaking glass.

More recently-introduced devices include those detectors which are activated by the sound of breaking glass within a specified distance. They are often fixed to the ceiling or walls adjacent to the area of glass being protected and are insensitive to other sounds such as passing traffic or accidental knocks. A similar form of acoustic detector is often used to protect strongrooms and is set to respond to airborne sounds resulting from a physical attack on the structure of the strongroom. These are usually set to be triggered off by sound at least 15 dB above ambient noise level.

Probably the most sophisticated glass detector is a direct development from the laminated security glass mentioned in the previous section. Within the laminations is included a special transparent conductive layer whose electrical resistance is predetermined. This layer is connected by electrodes to an analyser. When the glass is attacked, the resistance of the special layer is affected and the change is detected by the analyser which in turn triggers off the alarm system. Unlike the metallic foil solution, this protection cannot be seen by the assailant.

Vibration detectors are also used to give alarm of attack on other surfaces than glass. They are adhered to the surface they are protecting and are capable of ignoring normal mechanical vibration or shocks. Another form of detector meant to be attached to the protected structure is the rigid printed-circuit wiring detector. Consisting of conductors, not less than 1.3 mm and not more than 3.2 mm in size, adhered to a board substrate at 100 mm centres, this circuit is protected by a moisture-resistant coating and will generate an alarm when it is broken. The circuit side of the board is always set to face the protected area.

Movement detectors

The simplest types of internal movement detector are pressure pads under carpets or flooring and magnetic contacts on internal doors. These are the only forms of passive detector in this classification.

The weight of a person standing on the pressure pad will trigger the system. Usually 100 N is sufficient weight to produce an alarm. The pad's outer surface must be flexible, yet abrasion resistant; equivalent to 0.3 mm thick PVC sheet. Pressure pads can be usefully placed in internal doorways, on stair treads or as a back-up to window or door sensors.

More sophisticated detectors (Fig. 5.11) fall largely into four categories: those volumetric devices which respond to the Doppler effect (i.e. the movement of the intruder causes a response by interference with the radio or ultrasonic sound waves transmitted by the device), passive infra-red detectors which respond to the

Fig. 5.11 Hakuto International wide angle radar motion detector

different thermal radiation of a room when a moving person enters its surveillance field, active infra-red detectors which respond to the interruption of a beam of radiation between the detector and a receiver, and capacitive detectors.

Doppler effect detectors work best when the intruder's movement is towards or away from the device; the passive infra-red detector when the intruder passes across the device's field of observation. These detectors and the volumetric capacitive detector have an area of coverage which should be stated by the manufacturer. However with all these devices their positioning is vital. Inexpert siting can significantly reduce their area of coverage and alterations to the positions of objects in the room can also affect their performance. Each device should be fitted with a method of indication which allows the occupier to establish the area of cover before setting the system. BS 4737 sets out recommendations concerning the sensitivity of these detectors and it also suggests that a trial period of 7 days should be allowed before they are connected up to a direct police link, just to establish that false alarms are unlikely.

Beam interruption detectors are clearly most effective when positioned on recognised circulation routes which the intruder would find it difficult to avoid. BS 4737 recommends that they should operate if the beam is interrupted for 40 ms or more, but should not be activated if the interruption is less than 20 ms.

Capacitive proximity detectors are used to protect specific objects. They respond to a change (or rate of change) in capacitance resulting from the proximity (or touching) of the protected object by a person. Once again BS 4737 recommends a 7-day trial period before connecting to a direct police link.

Sometimes two types of detector are linked into one quite small unit. This is the case of the Gemini movement detector from Guardall which combines ultrasonic and passive infra-red detection techniques (see Fig. 5.12). These are often used with the IDI 200 multiplexed alarm system of sister company, Chubb Alarms. This means that one 4-wire cable can wire 16 zones, each with six different responses, and each zone being identified at the control unit.

Deliberately operated devices
These usually take the form of a push-button, similar to the personal attack button mentioned later, positioned in an unobtrusive, but easily reached, position close to a work station; e.g. beside a bank cashier. They can take two forms; the latching form which, once operated, will continue to operate until reset, and the non-latching type which stops operating when the stimulus is removed. Hand activated devices should need a pressure between 0.5 and 1.0 N and foot operated devices a pressure between 0.5 and 2.0 N. Such personal attack buttons can be included in domestic burglar alarm installations, when they are often positioned by the entrance door.

Control units

The heart of an intruder alarm system is the control unit. This receives the 'message' of an attack and triggers off the alarm sounder. In more complex systems it records the area of the attack and even operates a direct alarm facility to the local police force.

Fig. 5.12 Gemini dual technology movement detector from Guardall

The simplest form of control unit is a single zone unit in which all the alarm points are contained on the same indication zone. When the control unit is activated, all alarm points become active. These units are only used for the smallest of installations and today even small domestic installations tend to be two-zone systems which can be either wholly activated when the property is unoccupied or partially activated when it is occupied. An example of the convenience of this facility is the two-storey house in which the ground floor doors and windows are wired on to one alarm loop, while the less vulnerable upstairs windows are on a second loop. This allows the upstairs bedroom windows to be open on summer nights when the occupants are in bed, while still having full protection downstairs.

The control unit monitors the system to ensure that if there is any defect, immediate warning of the condition is given. It also provides a 24-hour protection against any attempt to tamper with the system. Many control units have a full-time personal attack facility, too, which operates whether the system is switched on or off. This is activated by pressing a personal attack button, often sited in domestic property beside the entrance door. The alarm will continue to sound until the button is reset. This facility is especially useful to the old and infirm or bedridden who may need to raise the alarm because of other emergencies as well as personal attack. Usually the control unit allows an adjustable delay to be programmed into the system to allow the owner of the property to set the alarm and leave the property without triggering off the system. A similar delay on entry is provided.

Control units normally operate off the mains electricity supply, but contain standby recharging batteries in case of mains failure.

There is a wide variety of control equipment from the simple one or two circuit, bell-only systems, to the complex microprocessor based controllers which monitor 80 or more detector circuits and which include other functions, such as recording events and automatic summoning of the police via the public telephone network. Often these more complex systems are linked to fire alarm control and other security systems and these will be discussed in detail in Chapter 10: *Integrated security systems*.

Alerting device

The sounder plays an important part in the intruder system. Firstly it acts as a deterrent to many would-be criminals; secondly its operation during a break-in will frequently cause the criminal to abort his attempt; and finally the noise aids the police to pinpoint the building under attack.

The sounder may be a bell or some form of siren horn. It can give a continuous or an intermittent sound (average output 70 dBA), provided in the latter case that it sounds at a frequency of 1 s on and 1 s off. Ideally it needs to be placed at least 27 m from the ground to give the best spread of sound, and to be inaccessible enough to avoid tampering. Many sounders also have an integral visual warning light to help the police to recognise which alarm is actually operating. This is particularly important when a number of neighbouring domestic properties all have intruder alarms.

Many alerting devices have anti-tamper mechanisms which trigger off the alarm when an attempt is made to interfere with the sounder. Some contain their own rechargeable batteries, so that they will sound even if the wiring to the unit is cut.

Self-contained intruder alarms

There are a number of self-contained intruder alarms on the market which are intended to cover individual rooms in a building. The intention of these devices is to give the intruder, having gained entry to the building, a nasty shock which may be sufficient to make him turn tail. They often work on the passive infra-red method of detecting changes in thermal radiation in the room caused by a person entering their surveillance area. When activated the integral sounder is set off. It will continue to sound for a predetermined period, after which the device will be automatically reset.

Often these units look rather similar to a stereo loudspeaker, they are connected to the mains and have a standby rechargeable battery which will give a considerable period of operation in the event of mains failure. They have an exit and entry delay period and some patterns have the facility to connect on remote intruder alarm sensors. Others contain integral flashing lights. This latter type is particularly useful to protect building site offices.

Other security devices for doors and windows

In addition to locks, which have been discussed in some detail at the beginning of this chapter, doors and windows can be fitted with a variety of other devices which will increase their security.

Robust bolts at the top and bottom of external doors increase the difficulty of forcing an entry. Surface mounted bolts on glass and wood panel doors are still highly vulnerable. They should be replaced by mortice security bolts. The problem is that for all doors to be bolted in this way, the property has to be occupied. If unoccupied, there will always be at least one door which is not manually bolted.

Many of the subsidiary items of door security, however, are specifically designed to protect the premises when they are occupied. For instance, one of the chief dangers can arise when the door is opened to a would-be intruder who then forces his way into the property. For this reason it is wise to be able to see who is on the other side of a solid front door before opening it. The door viewer (Judas window) is an ideal way of examining the visitor without advertising to him that he is being observed. Vision angles of up to 200° are possible with some patterns of door viewer. These devices are particularly desirable when the space outside the door is not overlooked or well-trafficked; for instance, a landing or corridor outside a flat's front door.

'Foot-in-the-door' attacks can be rendered less dangerous if the door is fitted with a security chain, or the even stronger door limiter. This latter device consists of a door mounted bracket, a frame mounted bracket and a robust arm running between the two. Door limiters are said to be capable of withstanding loads of up to 0.75 tonnes. What is more, they defeat attacks from bolt croppers. Both devices, however, allow the door to be opened sufficiently to ascertain the identity of the visitor, whilst still restricting the opening to a few centimetres.

Finally in this group of minor door security devices, it must be remembered that outward opening doors, because their hinges are exposed, are particularly vulnerable to attack. If their hinge pins can be removed, even a securely locked door can be prised open from its hinge side. The fixing of hinge bolts to the hinge edge of the door will overcome this weakness. Two bolts per door should be fitted, each within a few centimetres of the hinge.

Opening lights of windows should be fitted with window locks (either retaining the opening light itself or locking its catch). These should be operated by keys, so that the intruder cannot cut a small hole in the glass, put his hand through and release the catch or lock. He is forced into the much more noisy business of forming a large enough hole in the glass to climb through. This may well be sufficient deterrent to put off the opportunist thief.

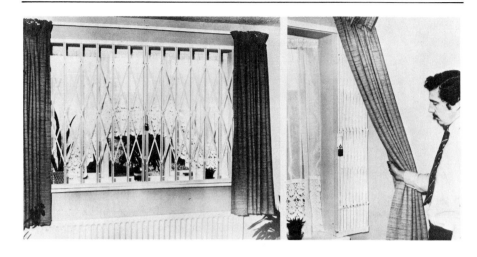

Fig. 5.13 Bolton Gates Xtraguard window grille

There are many types of window locks on the market for wood, metal or plastic windows. Also, do not forget the patio door. Locks for this type of window are now readily available.

When window security is particularly vital, special security shutters and grilles should be considered (Fig. 5.13). One of the neatest currently available is produced by the Bolton Gate Company. Called the Xtraguard, this grille is based on the lattice bar and picket system, runs on a top track fastened to the lintel which is completely concealed behind the curtain rail or pelmet in a domestic situation, and folds up into a space less than a fifth of its extended width.

Notes

1. BS 3621: 1980 *Specification for Thief-resistant Locks*
2. BS 6262: 1982 *Code of Practice; Glazing for Buildings*
3. BS 6206: 1981 *Specification for Impact Performance Requirements for Flat Safety Glass and Safety Plastics for use in Buildings*
4. BS 5544: 1978 *Specification for Anti-bandit Glazing (Glazing Resistant to Manual Attack*
5. BS 5051: Part 2: 1976 *Bullet-resistant Glazing for Interior Use*
6. BS 4737: Part 1; 1978 *Requirements for Systems with Audible Signalling only* Part 2; 1977 *Requirements for Systems with Remote Signalling only*

Chapter 6

Access control

The previous chapter dealt with keeping intruders out of a building and raising the alarm if an illegal entry were made; the present chapter concerns allowing approved people easy access to a building, or part of a building, while excluding everyone else. A simple form of this is the domestic entry control system in which the visitor presses a buzzer, speaks to the occupant of the building through a microphone/speaker system and identifies himself. The occupant then releases the lock on the door by remote control – usually by releasing an electric striker or operating an electric lock. A more sophisticated version of this system contains a closed-circuit television camera which allows the building owner to see who is at the door, before even letting the visitor know that there is anyone at home. In this way, if the occupier of the building does not wish to speak to the visitor, he need not (Fig. 6.1). These systems primarily give *defensive protection* (as defined in Chapter 1) because they include a locking system. In their more sophisticated form they also give *fail-safe protection* by raising the alarm in the event of an illegal entry or entry attempt.

Early forms of access control in industrial, commercial and multi-occupancy domestic property demanded the supervision of all entrance points to a particular building, area or site by a security guard who verified the identity of personnel as they passed in and out of the secure area and recorded entrance and exit times. This is clearly a labour intensive operation, and therefore very expensive and out of key with present labour-saving attitudes. Present systems are intended to be as far as possible automatic. Where security guards are necessary, these tend to be fewer in number and sited at a central location to which all entry systems supply a continuous stream of information.

In short, the modern access control system has been developed to reduce the cost of conventional access control, increase the amount of information supplied by the system and eliminate human error by the substitution of a completely mechanical surveillance and recording system.

Clearly, if access is to become largely a matter of 'self-service', each individual in an organisation needs to have a key or keys to allow access to all relevant areas. Also it is often desirable to have access recorded in much the same way as a security guard would record entrance and exits.

The complications that can result from this, using conventional locks and master

55

Fig. 6.1 Audio-visual entry system from Knobs and Knockers

key systems, can be almost insuperable. Also the desirability of personnel having pockets full of keys is questionable.

Imagine the laboratory technician driving into the car park of his employer's offices. If the system is entirely unmanned, he needs to unlock the barrier to the car park (low security rating), enter at least one of the outside doors of the office (medium security rating), walk through the office to the laboratory (high security rating) and enter an ultra-high security storage area within that laboratory. With a conventional master key system, our lab technician could no doubt be provided with a sub master key that could cover all these levels of security, but the likelihood is that such a sub master key might also give him access to areas of no concern to him and ones which might house activities with quite different security sensitivity to those with which he normally deals.

What is more, if he found his sub master key fitted another group of offices, to which he theoretically had no access, no record of his explorations need ever exist, if a normal master key access system applied.

Access control systems are designed to allow those persons having a need to enter various parts of the building to do so with a minimum of fuss, but to protect them, their property and their work from unauthorised interference. In addition, the entrance and exit to and from particularly security sensitive areas is accurately recorded, in case of the need to investigate security breaches.

One way of overcoming these problems is to impose magnetic or electronic codes on the keys or cards used to gain access. These codes need to match codes contained in the control system for the locks to work and, furthermore, because of the specialness of the coding, the cards have an individuality which permits movement records to be easily assembled.

Keyed access control

There are various key-based access control systems on the market, all of which depend on magnetically or electronically encoded keys. When these are inserted into a key reader and their codes are found to match those already programmed into the system, the doors are electrically unlocked. One interesting example of this type of system is the Knobset, joint development of Philips Business Systems and Salisbury Locks (Fig. 6.2).

Knobset comprises a Salisbury electrically-operated lock into which has been incorporated a Philips key reader. The insertion of a correctly encoded key into the reader is recorded at a central control point. A microswitch in the lock monitors the position of the pull-tongue and is linked to another switch in the door's leading edge which senses whether the door is open or closed. If the position of the tongue does not correspond to the open or closed position of the door, an alarm is set off. This eliminates the possibility of the tongue being taped back to keep the door open after an entry has been made. A third microswitch in the back plate replaces an exit pushbutton and monitors the turning of the knob to permit a valid exit. In other words, in the normal condition, entrance would be made from outside by a key, and exit by turning the knob. Alternatively a key reader can be incorporated on both entry and exit sides.

One of the benefits of this system is that the Philips reader need only be used on

Fig. 6.2 Philips Business Systems/Salisbury Lock Knobset

those doors where access control is required, while other doors can be fitted with Knobsets that look alike but have no reader fitted.

Philips has other electronic access control systems which are scaled to the size of installation required. They contain simple reprogramming facilities should the system security parameters change, constant monitoring of the system functions and automatic warning of malfunctions, tampering or invalid key use. All Philips' systems employ magnetically encoded nylon keys which carry no visible identification.

Kaba-20 security cylinder locks have already been mentioned in the last chapter. But the normal Kaba lock can now be combined with a highly developed electronic coding/de-coding system – Kaba-Cosmos.

Unlike magnetic systems, Kaba-Cosmos utilises an electronic code. When the system is switched on, normal Kaba-20 keyholders will be excluded from specific areas, only Kaba-Cosmos encoded keys operating the locks. Should a key be lost the electronic code can be quickly and simply changed and a new key issued. There is no need to replace the lock. Exact copying of the Kaba-20 key is difficult enough, but with the electronic code the task becomes virtually impossible. Failure of the mains electricity can mean that an electronic system becomes ineffective unless standby batteries are installed. The Kaba-20 mechanical security system will, however, remain effective.

The Cosmos electronic unit monitors the operation of the locks and it can be programmed to switch the Cosmos function on and off at specific times of the day or night.

A system which is more like a traditional master key system but which employs plastic or stainless steel encoded cards, is the Corkey method from Corkey Control Systems (UK) (Fig. 6.3). The most distinctive feature of this system is the speed

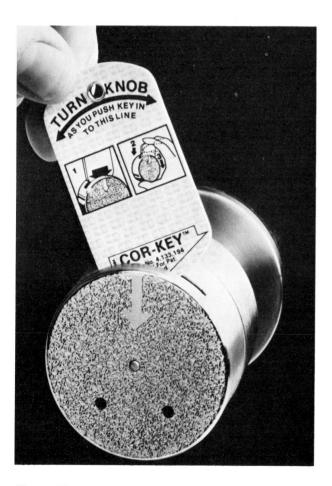

Fig. 6.3 The Corkey system being operated

with which the locks can be remastered. The lock contains three independent magnetic codes. Two of these codes can be changed as many times as required without disassembling the lock. The third code determines in which building, floor and door the lock is located. The code on the key has to match those on the lock before the lock can be operated. The building owner is supplied with an encoding and rekeying kit containing a code gun. This is used, 'firing' through a code format card, to code or reformat the Corkeys or the locks. It is possible for the building owner, very easily, to rejig the whole of his building's locking arrangements. Almost more importantly, in the event of a lost Corkey, the lock codes can be modified and a new Corkey produced within minutes.

Card access systems

At the heart of every card access system is a plastic card, the size and shape of a credit card. This contains an unbreakable magnetic command code which is permanently fixed within the card. The code is unique and cannot be copied, altered or erased. If the card is defaced – the only alteration that can be made to it – the system will not accept it. The card has no external magnetic field and therefore does not affect other magnetic media.

The card is inserted into a reader at each entrance or doorway where access control is needed. If the card contains an approved code, the door will be unlocked electrically, or the barrier will be raised, or the turnstile become free to revolve (Fig. 6.4).

There is considerable flexibility within card access systems to allow them to be scaled to the requirements of the particular building. The method of encoding the card, too, can affect the capacity and complication of the readers. For instance, it is said that the Wiegand Pulse Generating Effect used in encoding Cardkey Securiti-Cards has increased this company's range and the simplicity of its readers.

Off-line installations consist of individual readers, each controlling one access point. These are usually arranged so that their control circuitry is located on the inside of the protected area, thus giving maximum security (Fig. 6.5). The most basic reader usually contains a preprogrammed range of valid card numbers with a card validation option. More sophisticated access controllers have a microprocessor-based control unit, situated in a secure location up to 10 m away from the reader. This contains the system's card memory and the unit is programmable by the building owner.

For an added level of security, an integral keyboard is sometimes incorporated into the reader with which the cardholder has to enter a memorised 4-digit Personal Identity Number (a PIN). This number and the card code have to correspond to the codes entered into the system's card memory (Fig. 6.6). Codes can be altered periodically, enabling management to exercise discretionary control. The readers are managed by a microprocessor-based control unit in a secure location near the reader. Some systems are capable of being programmed to prohibit entry during specific time periods.

Fig. 6.4 The Yaletronic self-contained card operated lock

These off-line, stand-alone devices can often be fitted with extra alarm facilities to warn of unauthorised and duress entry attempts. Repeated incorrect PIN entries will trigger an alarm; in addition, an alarm will be raised in the event of a cardholder being forced to enter a security area with the intruder, merely by the cardholder punching a special duress code into the reader.

For the larger, more sophisticated security system, *on-line* equipment is needed with centralised control and recording facilities (Fig. 6.7). The equipment for a centralised system is similar to that used in off-line installations (i.e. readers and control units) but to this is now added the computerised central controller. It is this equipment's memory which now governs the card capacity of the system, not the memory of the readers' control units. Additional protective systems can also be assigned by the central controller – such as restrictions on multiple use, anti-passback control and time/status level inhibitions.

enough for # of users.   Benefits of a centralised
                           System. Greater flexibility.
                      Reduction of patrolling

61

Fig. 6.5 A compact card reader in the Chubb Alarms Entacard M300 system. It may operate as a stand-alone unit with up to 300 coded cards, or linked to the central system

Determined by Interface

Access levels are established for each personnel group. The validity of each access level can be restricted according to the time of the day or week, rendering its cards invalid outside specified time zones. The anti-passback option avoids a card, belonging to one person who has already entered a security area, being passed back for use by a non-cardholder to enter the security area behind the true cardholder. In this case individual readers are designated 'in' and 'out' units. Each card number is then monitored as being either in or out. Once in, a card is not valid for another inward movement until it has passed out through an 'out' reader.

Other options include a lift control. This allows the access of certain cardholding groups to be prohibited from some levels in multi-storey buildings. The cardholder needs to select the floor desired on the lift's pushbutton panel, and then insert his card into the reader. If his card is not validated for the floor selected, the lift will not move. Error annunciation is a feature which triggers off a discreet alarm at the

62

Boolean

Fig. 6.6 Cardkey Systems' D30 access control system combining keyboard code and encoded card control

central controller if anyone enters an incorrect code more than a specified number of times. Also the duress alarm, referred to earlier, will activate a discreet alarm at the central controller of an in-line installation, thus allowing the victim and intruder to pass into the security area without the intruder being made aware that an alarm has been raised.

The logging of personnel movements can have other benefits. It can be used as an alternative to clocking on and clocking off for hourly paid staff, and it is particularly useful where flexitime is being implemented. Some systems, notably the MD4000 system of Cardkey Systems (Fig. 6.8), are geared up for all the standard attendance management techniques, including fixed and flexible working hours plus overtime and can be easily tailored to individual company requirements. It can be linked directly to the payroll system and can report automatically on such items as absenteeism or lateness.

In an emergency many on-line card access systems print out a list of cardholders by name, giving their current locations within the building. The possibilities are clearly endless. In fact card access systems often form the basis of a series of

Fig. 6.7 Cardkey Systems' D2000 system controlling up to 4000 programmable Cardkeys. It also can control other features of an integrated security system, such as alarms and closed-circuit television

Fig. 6.8 Cardkey Systems' MD4000 attendance recording system

Fig. 6.9 Rapid Access system being negotiated without the need for hand operation

management and surveillance functions, such as monitoring intruder alarm and fire alarm systems, regulating air conditioning, automatic switching of lights and general energy management functions. These systems will be discussed in Chapter 10 when integrated security systems are considered.

telligent Buildings. — extension.
More Interfaces.

9 if no-one in building
for 72hrs turn off
heating.

Fig. 6.10 Rapid Access electronic tag

Electronic access tags

A new development in access systems eliminates the need to present a card to a reader. In effect, this is a 'no-hands' system which allows passage through turnstiles or doorways without the person actually having to do anything at all, merely carry an electronic tag (Fig. 6.9).

The system, introduced by Eureka Systems of Slough, is called Rapid Access and depends on a small plastic tag, little bigger than a postage stamp, each of which is battery-powered and programmed with its own identity code (Fig. 6.10). These automatically 'talk' to electronic sensors, telling them to open doors or barriers. They have a battery life of about 5 years and can be carried anywhere on the person, or in a handbag or briefcase.

The code identifies the tag holder and also specifies to what locations, at what times and for what periods access is permitted. This information is transmitted on

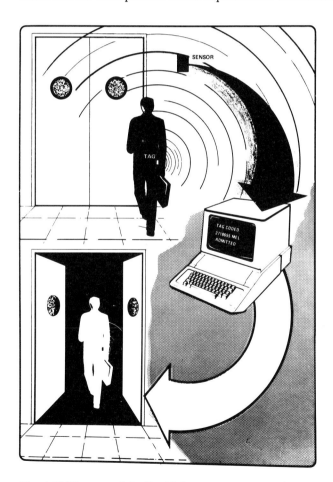

Fig. 6.11 Diagram of the Rapid Access system operation

command to door or barrier sensors linked to microprocessors which are programmed to control a variety of routine security functions (Fig. 6.11).

Tag codes cannot be emulated and the codes of tags lost or stolen can be instantly eliminated from the system memory. Intruders trying to gain unauthorised entry will be detected immediately. The system can be even linked to cctv cameras to record the event. Sensors can be installed unobtrusively behind most building materials without interrupting the signal.

All the more sophisticated access systems, whether card or electronic, have the potential to carry out many more functions than merely control access. For this reason they form the basis of most integrated security systems discussed in Chapter 10.

Chapter 7

Fire detection and alarm

Fire protection is a subject that straddles the fine line between security and safety. It has been decided to include fire detection and alarm equipment in this book because these subjects are closely related to similar equipment which protects against illegal entry. In fact, in fully integrated protection systems, equipment for each function can be included on the same control system – as well as the manipulation of other building functions such as access control and energy management. Other aspects of fire protection, such as means of escape, fire resistance of elements of structure, escape routes and fire fighting equipment have not been included. These subjects are independent of security and, indeed, are major subjects in their own right.

There is another reason that connects fire detection and alarm more closely to security than would necessarily appear at first sight. Fire is often the by-product of another crime, such as vandalism. School fires, for instance, are usually the result of the fire-raising activities of vandals. This is becoming an increasing problem. School fires almost trebled between 1969 and 1974, causing the Department of Education and Science to call for the upgrading in the provision of fire stops and fire breaks and the Fire Protection Association to recommend that automatic fire alarm systems should be fitted in all schools.

The nature of fire

Every year fire causes loss of life, serious injury and considerable damage to property. An estimate of the annual bill for fire damage in the UK in 1981 came to over £350,000,000. In 1980 fire brigades attended over 352,000 outbreaks; while in the same year 1035 people lost their lives and 8770 received injuries as a result of fires. The majority of fires occur in domestic property; of incidents in other types of property, a high proportion occur when the building is unoccupied, between the hours of 6 pm and 6 am, and therefore when there is no one around to raise the alarm. In these circumstances, although life is possibly not endangered, property damage can be often more extensive due to the delay in calling the fire brigade. Only an efficient automatic early-warning alarm system can reduce the fire loss in these conditions. A study of the records of three fire brigade areas has suggested that the general installation of such systems could have reduced the losses by a percentage that varied from 50 to 90%.

Cooking appliances cause a large percentage of domestic fires, while in other types of building three major causes of fires have been identified:

1. Malicious ignition.
2. Failure, misuse or lack of maintenance of electrical equipment.
3. Causes directly attributable to smoking.

In a post-war Building Study, dated 1952, buildings were 'fire graded' and it was recommended that fire alarms should be installed in all buildings (other than factories) which complied with one of the following criteria:

1. A single storey building with more than 100 occupants.
2. A building with more than 60 occupants above ground floor level.
3. A building of abnormal fire risk irrespective of occupancy.

Clearly these criteria were based more on the risk to life than on the damage to property. Today, the building owner's insurance company would tend to place greater emphasis on minimising property damage by the early raising of an alarm than did the writers of the Building Study.

There are two methods of initiating a fire alarm. People can raise the alarm, or warning can be given automatically by a fire detector sensing one of the products of combustion and setting off the alarm electronically.

During a fire, heat, visible and invisible combustion gases and radiation are produced. Each of these products of combustion can be sensed automatically by one or other of the types of fire detector available. The problem is that not all fires are the same. The character of a fire depends on what is being burned, causing one or other of the products of combustion to dominate – particularly during those vital early minutes when the fire is taking hold and the alarm needs to be raised. As a result, no single type of detector is effective at giving an early warning of every type of fire.

Heat emission from some fires in their early stages can be quite small and the temperature rise slow; in other cases the rate of temperature rise can be swift. Similarly, some fires begin by smouldering, slowly producing dense quantities of smoke; while others are clean-burning and produce 'invisible smoke' – tiny particles called aerosols. Other fires produce flame right from the beginning, emitting high levels of radiation.

As we shall see later in this chapter, there are a number of detectors which react to each of the characteristics of combustion: heat detectors sense an abnormal temperature rise or the reaching of a predetermined critical temperature; smoke detectors either use the Tyndall principle of light scatter from smoke particles operating a photosensitive device, or an ionisation chamber which senses the aerosols from a clean-burning fire; and finally radiation detectors are sensitive to infra-red or ultraviolet radiation from solvent fires and the like.

Fire is an insidious killer. Not only does it kill by burning, but more often as a result of asphixiation or poisoning caused by the gases, visible and invisible, given off during burning. In fact, with regard to smoke, BS 5839: Part 1: 1980[1] points out another problem. Often a relatively small patch of dense smoke on a safe escape route can inhibit people from making their escape down it. Many tragic deaths have been recorded where people's natural reticence to enter a patch of smoke has inhibited them from making their bid for safety, when clear air lay only a few metres beyond the smoke. BS 5839 states that generally people will not make their escape through smoke when their visibility is reduced to 10 m or below. This is particularly true when the occupants of the building do not know the layout of the escape routes, e.g. shoppers in a department store or casual occupants of public buildings. As a result, alarm systems should give a sufficiently early warning to allow occupants of the building to make their escape before the smoke on the escape routes has reduced visibility to below 20 m.

Types of system

Fire alarm systems fall into two categories – manual and automatic.

The manual system, at its simplest consists of a fire bell or other hand operated sounder. More usually today it is an electric system consisting of call points, of which the break-glass call point is the most familiar example. These are situated at strategic positions throughout the building, usually related to the escape routes. People are usually the most efficient fire detectors, assuming they are awake, active and mentally alert. Call points should be situated so that the maximum distance to be travelled from any place in the building to a call point is 30 m; obvious locations being on escape routes and staircases. When activated, these call points cause the control equipment to set off the alarm sounder.

The automatic system consists of a series of automatic fire detectors spaced throughout the building according to recommendations which will be given later in this chapter. These are sensitive to smoke, heat or radiation and they, via the control and indicating equipment, activate the alarm.

The manual system will normally give adequate protection in a building which is fully occupied by alert and active people. In fact, in these circumstances it is likely that the sense of smell of the occupants of the building is a more effective early warning system than automatic fire detectors. However, when the building is unoccupied, partially occupied, or occupied by handicapped, infirm or sleeping people, an automatic system is essential. It may well be that a combination of both systems will prove the most effective solution. In this case manual call points can be included on the automatic system.

It should be remembered that the purpose of any fire alarm system is to prevent loss of life and minimise damage to property. This is achieved most efficiently when the earliest possible notification of an outbreak of fire is given. The equipment should be chosen and sited with this object in mind.

In the interests of reliability, it is best that the number of circuit elements in a fire alarm system be kept to a minimum. The call points or detectors are usually solid state devices that are normally electrically open or closed – a condition which is reversed when the point is activated. The message is then conveyed by a simple circuit (or the breaking of a circuit) to the control and indicating equipment; from there the message is relayed by a number of simple means to the fire sounders, fixed fire extinguishing systems, fire doors, ventilation system, etc. The fire alarm system should also automatically register any fault which develops within itself. A cable disconnection in a simple 'open' circuit system or a cable short-circuit in a 'closed' system would, however, remain undetected until the routine testing of the installation. Equally a short-circuit in an 'open' circuit system or a cable disconnection in a 'closed' system would give a false alarm. In either case, regular routine testing is important. Also, the inclusion of a fault relay or its equivalent to each detector/call point circuit will automatically give indication of a cable fault without giving a false alarm. A fully self-monitoring system is possible with, however, additional complexities which can themselves introduce greater chances of defects occurring. This subject is extensively discussed in BS 5839: Part 1: 1980.

The protected area of the building should be divided into zones in order that any alarm gives a clear and unambiguous indication on the control board of where the alarm originated. Each zone should be readily accessible from the circulation areas and preferably one zone should not have to be crossed to gain entry to another zone.

BS 5839: Part 1 lays down certain requirements for the sizing of zones:

1. The floor area of each zone should not exceed 2000 m².
2. Each zone should not extend beyond a single fire compartment.
3. It should normally be restricted to one floor of a multi-storied building, except where the zone consists of a stair well or lift well, or in the case of a small building with a total floor area of less than 300 m².
4. It should be resticted to below 2000 m² when easy visibility of the precise location of a fire is restricted by racking or partitioning. In this case the distance that has to be travelled to determine visually the position of the fire within the zone is restriced to 30 m.

The Standard should be consulted for amplification of these guidelines.

Fire alarm systems should be powered, in the words of BS 5839: Part 1, 'sufficient to supply the largest load likely to be placed upon them and should be such that the reliability of the system is not appreciably reduced by power supply failures'. This means in effect that the supply will normally be from the mains with sufficient battery back-up to ensure the system is maintained for at least 24 hours (plus 30 minutes evacuation warning time) after power failure. There is a distinction made in the Standard between systems intended to protect life and those protecting property; and whether the building is continuously occupied or not. The central criteria, though, are that the supply should be maintained for at least 24 hours after the mains failure has been signalled to the occupants, or some remote and continuously manned station. After that 24-hour period, assuming the mains supply has not been reinstated, the batteries should have enough remaining power to sound an evacuation alarm for 30 minutes.

Standby batteries should have a life of at least 4 years and should be equipped with a charger that will recharge the spent batteries within 48 hours of total discharge. Automatic start emergency generators can offer an alternative to batteries on some systems. In the case of automatic systems, the power supply needs to be sufficient to power all alarm sounders simultaneously, plus the detectors working on a proportion of the zones. On a manual system similar conditions apply, without the need to power detectors. Also on manual installations in small (below 300 m² floor area) buildings, standby batteries are not considered by BS 5839: Part 1 to be essential.

Self-contained (single point) smoke and heat detectors which comply with BS 5446: Part 1 are available. These may be wholly mains operated, mains operated with rechargeable secondary batteries, or operated by primary batteries. These stand-alone devices will be discussed later in this chapter.

Type of fire detector

Fire detectors are designed to detect heat, smoke or radiation; each type contains two sub-types. No one type of detector is most suitable for all applications and the final choice of detector will depend on the individual circumstances. Table 7.1 summarises the types of detector available and their major characteristics.

All detectors have to distinguish between normal conditions in their areas of surveillance and a fire condition. What is more, their response to an abnormal condition must be as rapid as possible. Some types of detector have a quicker response to certain fires than to others and it may be necessary to use more than one type of detector in installations in buildings containing differently burning materials. For instance, a slowly smouldering fire will probably activate a smoke detector before a heat detector, whereas a fire which evolves little smoke should trigger off a heat detector first and a flammable liquid fire, a radiation detector.

The following is a summary of the behaviour of the various detectors.

Heat detectors

These are either of the 'fixed-temperature' or 'rate-of-rise' type, or a combination of both. Fixed-temperature detectors are less suitable in areas with low ambient temperatures or where temperatures may vary slowly over a wide range. Combined fixed-temperature and rate-of-rise detectors are less suitable where the ambient temperature may vary over short periods. Where very high temperatures are likely, detectors complying with BS 5445: Part 8² should be used.

Generally heat detectors are suitable for most internal locations, except in areas (like computer rooms) where large losses could be caused by small fires. False alarms are most commonly caused by abnormal temperature rises caused by heating equipment, industrial processes or sunshine. Siting of heat detectors should be made with care to avoid these problems, alternatively detectors with higher temperature settings should be used.

Table 7.1 Types of fire detector — main characteristics

Type	Sub-type	Activated by —	Mode of operation	Standards applying
Heat detectors	Point detector	Hot gas immediately adjacent	(a) Fixed temperature (static) elements; and/or	(a) or (a) plus (b) detectors comply with BS 5445: Part 5 & 8
	Line detector	Hot gas anywhere along the detector line	(b) Rate-of-rise temperature element	Detectors with (b) alone do not comply and should not be used
Smoke detectors	Ionization chamber detector (point type)	Smoke particles restricting flow of current through an ionization chamber	Note: Sampling detectors take air from several of positions to a point smoke detector	BS 5446: Part 1 covers residential applications; BS 5445: Part 7 for industrial and commercial. The former is adequate when latter
	Optical detector (point or line)	Scattering or absorption of light by smoke particles in a light beam	Some can also detect thermal turbulence	similar to domestic. Not covered at present by standard. Can be safely used when approved by recognised body
Radiation (flame) detectors	Ultra-violet type	U.V. radiation emitted from flames in frequency range 220 – 270 nm	Radiation-sensitive cells which 'see' the fire directly or its reflection in mirrors	*Other comments:* Do not respond to gas/oxygen flames, may respond to gas fire if gas contaminated or badly mixed. Are sun-blind
	Infra-red type	I.R. radiation with a flicker frequency between 5 to 50 Hz		Newly introduced sun-blind I.R. detectors are not disturbed by sunlight

Smoke detectors

Broadly these detectors give a faster response than heat detectors, but are more prone to give false alarms. Ionisation chamber smoke detectors respond quickly to small particles produced in clean-burning fires; less quickly to optically dense smoke created in smouldering fires and those involving PVC. Optical smoke detectors are better for these types of fire. Ionisation chamber detectors are less likely to give a false alarm with tobacco smoke than optical detectors.

Generally smoke detectors which incorporate thermal turbulence sensors are the only smoke detectors to react to alcohol and other clean-burning liquid fires, but this need not necessarily be a serious drawback as most fires involve other combustible materials at an early stage and these contaminants cause smoke to form. Combining optical beam detectors and thermal turbulence detectors is the ideal solution for this type of fire.

Smoke detectors with thermal turbulence sensors may be unsatisfactory above some blower heaters and in areas housing some industrial processes which result in considerable waste heat.

No type of smoke detector is recommended where industrial processes produce smoke or fumes in sufficient quantities to trigger off the detectors. False alarms are most usually caused by dust accumulations, steam or condensation, engine exhausts and very fast airflow conditions such as those experienced in some warehouses in windy conditions.

Radiation (flame) detectors

These detectors give the most speedy warning of clean-burning fires so long as there is an unobstructed path between the fire and the detector. Because of their quick response at long range, they are particularly useful in outdoor applications, such as in timber yards, or the general surveillance of large open areas in warehouses and storage buildings. They are particularly useful in high buildings and for special monitoring of critical areas where fire could spread rapidly; e.g. at pumps and valves or pipework containing flammable liquids.

False alarms can be given by ultraviolet detectors responding to radiation from ultraviolet lamps, cutting and welding operations and quartz halogen lamps not shielded with a glass cover. Sunlight, however, does not activate these detectors. The flicker sensitivity which is built into infra-red detectors can be simulated by the ripples of sunlight on a pool of water or the revolution of a fan in front of sunlight or a very hot body.

Flame detectors are often used in hazardous locations, such as in the oil or petroleum industries. The ultraviolet detector has a larger power requirement (typically 0.5 W) than an infra-red detector, and hence has to be housed in a flameproof enclosure, adding to its bulk and expense. An infra-red detector, on the other hand, with a power requirement of less than 2.5 mW, can be made intrinsically safe, resulting in a less cumbersome detector. Infra-red detectors have twice the sensing range of ultraviolet detectors; they are also extremely tolerant of optical contamination on the detector's lens. However, because ultraviolet detectors are solar blind and infra-red detectors can be disturbed by sunshine, the ultravoilet detectors, until recently, afforded considerable advantages.

Flame detectors clearly have to discriminate between real flame and deceptive phenomena which may cause false alarms. In the past it has sometimes been necessary to use double detector systems; e.g. two ultravoilet detectors used in combination, the first surveying the risk area, the second the general surroundings. When the risk area detector output considerably exceeded that of the other detector an alarm was given. Infra-red detectors with a two sensor arrangement have also been used, each sensor being 'tuned' to a different part of the infra-red spectrum. This avoided this type of detector becoming confused by interference from solar radiation. Both methods obviously carry a substantial cost penalty.

At least one company (AFA-Minerva) has at last developed a solar-blind infra-red detector which makes twin sensor devices unnecessary. This removes a major shortcoming of infra-red detectors and allows their advantages to be fully realised. Solar blindness is achieved by using a single pyroelectric sensor, coupled to a special narrow-band optical filter which permits the detector only to operate at the 4.4 micron wavelength, where solar radiation is reduced by CO^2 absorption, but at which flame radiation peaks.

Siting of detectors

The positioning of fire detectors is a complex subject, being affected by a number of considerations, such as the type of detector, the size and shape of the building and its ceiling heights. For instance, flame detectors operate more effectively in tall, open interior spaces (as they do also in open external areas), and within prescribed limits the distance from the fire to the detector is not a drawback provided that the detector can 'see' the fire, or its reflection. Smoke and heat detectors, on the other hand, take longer to react in tall rooms and are ineffective in most external locations. Under low ceilings care in the siting of smoke detectors is necessary to ensure against false alarms being induced by tobacco smoke or other small smoke-raising sources. Optical beam smoke detectors may generally be used at greater ceiling heights than the equivalent point-type detector.

Ceilings which are not flat or are made up of various levels will need extra care in the layout of detectors, depending on the slope of the ceiling or the proportion of raised areas in relation to the overall floor area of the room. When downstand obstructions, such as beams or ducting, are of greater depth than 10% of the ceiling height, they need to be considered as walls and each side of the downstand treated as separate rooms.

All these, and other, considerations are discussed at length in BS 5839: Part 1. Its general recommendations concerning the spacing, positioning and use of various types of detector are summarised in Table 7.2.

It should be remembered that there are some special areas which need even greater care in the selection of some types of detector; for instance, heat detectors in

Table 7.2 Guide dimensions in positioning fire detectors

	Point-type heat detector	Point-type smoke detector	Line-type heat detector (point response)	Integr. line-type heat detector	Optical beam smoke detector and turbulence detector	Radiation detector
Spacing (m)	5.3*	7.5*	5.3	5.0 perp. to beam	7.0 perp. to	Must be able to 'see' the fire or its reflection
Area (m²)	50	100	—	—	—	
Min. distance to wall (mm)	500	500	500	500	500	
			not more than 3 m of beam within this distance			
Element to ceiling (mm)	Max 150 Min 25	Max 600 Min 25	Max 150 Min 25	Max 150 Min 25	Max 600 Min 25	
Ceiling hts: general (m)	Grde 1: 9.0† Grde 2: 7.5† Grde 3: 6.0†	10.5 High temp. type 6.0	—	—	—	
Ceiling hts: higher lmts (m)	Grde 1: 13.5† Grde 2: 12.0† Grde 3: 10.5†	15.0 High temp. type 10.5	—	—	—	
Ht. of beam (m)	—	—	—	—	Max 25 Min 2.7	
Dist. between beams (m)	—	—	—	—	Max 14	
Beam length (m)	—	—	—	—	Max 100 Min 10	
Beam to flat ceiling (mm)	—	—	—	—	Max 600 Min 300	
Beam to parallel wall (m)	—	—	—	—	Max 8	

*In corridors (widths below 5 m) these dimensions can be increased
†Grades defined in BS 5445: Part 5

77

high-temperature areas or ones in which the ambient temperature is subject to fluctuations due to the processes they contain.

In the interests of protecting life, special attention needs to be given to circulation areas and escape routes. These should be covered by smoke detectors that are sensitive to all types of combustion gases. Heat detectors are not suitable for these areas as slow-burning fires often do not activate them until an unacceptable level of smoke has been reached in the corridors, thus preventing escape.

As well as detectors in corridors, each room (except for toilets) opening onto a staircase should be covered by a detector. In addition, a detector should be positioned at the head of each staircase and at landing levels at vertical intervals not greater than 10.5 m.

Control and indicating equipment

All control and indicating equipment for manual and automatic fire alarm systems should comply with the requirements of BS 3116: Part 4[3]. This equipment acts as an interface between the call point or detector and the audible or visual alarm devices and is responsible for activating these alarms. It may also operate other subsidiary equipment in the event of fire, like closing smoke stop doors, switching on normal lights on escape routes or signalling the alarm to a remote station or fire brigade.

Control equipment, except for that in single-zone buildings, should indicate the zone in which the alarm originated. Each zone should be clearly defined on the equipment so that the fire brigade, without prior knowledge of the layout of the building, can quickly discover the position of the fire. There are a number of methods of doing this. In very large buildings, sectors (groups of zones) can be defined. Sometimes the main control equipment merely indicates the sector in which the fire originated, while a subsidiary panel in each sector indicates the zone. Often a block plan or mimic diagram of the building showing its sectors and zones is permanently mounted on the control equipment.

The control equipment should also give warning of failure in the system by *both* an audible sounder *and* a visible indication on the equipment. Such a warning should be activated by failure of the power supply, standby power supply, battery-charging equipment or the disconnection or failure of any part of the system. The removal of the fault should automatically reset the fault-warning system.

Fire alarm control systems can form part of an integrated control system, including other functions, such as intruder alarms, access control and even energy management. This type of equipment is discussed in Chapter 10.

In a manual system, the sounders, once activated, should continue to function until manually shut off. This action should activate an audible signal at the control equipment (possibly the same signal as warns of a fault) which should continue until the fire alarm system is once more manually reset. It should be possible to reactivate the alarm, if necessary, at the indicator board. All this is to avoid the accidental switching off of an alarm prematurely, or a failure to reset the general alarm system after an alarm.

All manual controls should clearly indicate their function to avoid inadvertent operation and access to control equipment should be restricted to a small number of authorised personnel to avoid tampering or misuse.

Audible and visual alarms

The control equipment, having received a signal from a fire detector or a manual call point, activates the alarms. These usually take the form of bells or sirens; i.e. alarm sounders. Visual alarms, like rotating beacons or gas discharge lamps, should generally not be used, except in special circumstances (where noise levels are very high, or the occupants of the building are deaf) when they are usually used in addition to, and not instead of, audible alarms.

The alarm sounders discussed in this section do not include integral fault-warning alarms which have been dealt with in the previous section.

Fire alarm sounders should produce an alarm noise in the frequency range 500 to 1000 Hz, this being the most generally appreciated range and one which is attenuated less by partitions and building structure than higher frequencies.

Minimum sound levels should be 65 dB(A) or 5 dB(A) more than any persistent background noise in the building. In premises where people are sleeping, the minimum sound level should be raised to 75 dB(A) with sufficient allowance being made for the attenuation of partitions and doors. As the door is usually the point of weakest attenuation, these can be taken as a guide to the sound reduction of the partition; i.e. approximately 20 dB for normal single doors and 30 dB for fire doors. Thus it is unlikely a sounder is going to be effective in the terms set out above if its noise has to travel through more than one wall. At least one sounder should be positioned in each fire compartment.

Damage to hearing during the periods likely to be experienced in an alarm condition is unlikely up to a level of 120dB(A). In noisy locations where sound levels above this might be necessary, visual alarms may be used.

Fire alarm sounders should not perform any other function except that of warning of a fire. If, however, the building is fitted with an intercommunication or public address system, this can be used to convey an alarm. The provisos are: the alarm must be automatically and simultaneously transmitted to all areas; it must take priority over all other use of the system, automatically deadening all microphones; and there should be some indication of a fault on the system, if the alarm system has no control and indicating equipment.

The primary principle of any alarm system is that the sounders should continue to sound after the alarm has been given until normal conditions are restored. Under certain circumstances a manual silencing device can be installed to limit an alarm to a control sounder. Also in some large installations and high-rise buildings, it may be desirable to evacuate those at greatest risk first. In this case a two-stage alarm can be used, whereby an evacuation alarm is given in the high risk area, together with a standby warning in other areas. This and other detailed aspects of sounder installation are given in BS 5839: Part 1.

Automatic connection to fire brigade

Direct connection between the fire alarm installation and the local fire brigade may be possible, although this facility is becoming rare and is usually reserved for major risk cases. Alternatively, a connection may be made to a constantly manned commercial central fire alarm station with direct telephone connection to the fire brigade, or other similar methods. All these systems involve the renting of British Telecom lines and equipment for transmitting and receiving the electrical signal. The installation must be monitored and faults should be automatically indicated.

Other systems involve using the public switched telephone network and automatic special number dialling, a 999 Autodialler which plays a recorded message, or a British Telecom 'Alarm-by-carrier' service in which the alarm is transmitted to a special terminal at the fire brigade control room by conventional telephone exchange lines.

The object of any of these systems is to achieve the most speedy response from the fire brigade possible and early consultation with the local brigade is essential during the design of the installation to ensure the most effective choice is made.

Self-contained alarm systems

There are, as mentioned earlier, a group of self-contained detector/alarms which can be connected to the mains, powered by the mains plus a secondary rechargeable battery, or solely powered by a primary battery. These devices can be of the heat- or smoke-sensing type, and contain both the sensing device and the alarm sounder (Fig. 7.1). They are clearly most appropriate for use in the home or small

Fig. 7.1 Nu-Swift self-contained alarm

Fig. 7.2 Queensgate Shopping Centre, Peterborough

commercial premises. In some types of equipment a certain number of detectors can be wired together so that if one detector senses a fire, the sounders on all detectors will be actuated.

Conclusions and case studies

The whole business of the selection of appropriate equipment and the design of the best fire detection and alarm system for a building, particularly a complex building, is clearly work requiring skill and possibly the aid of one of the many specialists in the field. These are often commercial organisations which produce the equipment for such installations and back up their products with a complete design service. They also will undertake the installation of the system, its commissioning and its maintenance for a fixed annual fee. They provide a 24-hour, 7-day-a-week emergency service which can prove invaluable in the event of problems appearing in the system.

Designers should bear in mind that the size of their clients' insurance premiums may well depend upon how satisfied their insurance companies are with the general fire protection systems installed in the building, as well as with its fire fighting equipment and other aspects of its design. It is therefore wise to consult the insurance company at an early stage. This may well save the client's money in the long run.

81

In conclusion, two recent installations, each presenting its own special problems, are described in the hope that they will help to illustrate the complexities involved in major installations and the way these installations often interface with automatic fire extinguishing and other protection and environmental systems.

Fig. 7.3 The Tann Synchronome CMS 3000 control panel

Queensgate Centre, Peterborough

This development covers 17 acres in the heart of the city and consists of an enclosed shopping centre with five major retail stores, a supermarket, 97 retail shop units, a car park and a bus station (Fig. 7.2).

A custom-made automatic fire detection and alarm system, manufactured by Tann Synchronome, has been installed to protect this multi-level development. The 60-zone system is based around twelve CMS 3000 control panels (Fig. 7.3) which interface with a Serck computer controlling all other management functions within the public and maintenance areas – functions like security, mechanical plant, gas monitoring, air conditioning, heating and lighting.

Each CMS fire control panel monitors a section of the building, divided into zones. There are three separate fire officer control panels (Fig. 7.4); two of which are situated at two of the main entrances to the centre and the third in the central control room. These panels provide indications and controls for the sprinkler valves, fan units and smoke vents around the centre. These devices are normally in automatic operation but they can be subject to manual override if thought necessary by the fire officer. An intercom system at each fire officer control panel enables two-way speech between each panel and the central control room.

The trigger devices for the system comprise 512 smoke detectors, four heat detectors and 50 manual call points.

Fig. 7.4 Tann Synchronome's fire officer control panels with intercommunication facility

All the retail shops can be incorporated into the main system as required, each shop becoming a fresh zone. At the time of writing 80 of the leasing companies have been linked up.

Cape Hill Brewery, Mitchells & Butler, Smethwick

A new fire detection and alarm system, manufactured by Gent, has recently been installed in and around the new computer suite which is located in a former wine and spirit bond store of this brewery.

In the normally occupied areas of the building 12 manual call points, two heat detectors and 33 ionisation type smoke detectors are intended to initiate the alarm; in normally unoccupied areas 14 manual call points, 32 smoke detectors and one heat detector perform a similar function. The heart of the system is a 14-zone indication/control panel which not only activates the sounders in the event of fire, but automatically initiates a gaseous fire extinguishing system in the computer suite.

The latter action only occurs if fire is suspected in the computer suite, and at least one detector in both computer room zones has signalled a fire. The gas used is Halon 1301, which is colourless, odourless and non-toxic. It is automatically released to extinguish the fire by means of catalytic reaction. On an alarm being signalled, a special sounder operates during a delay period long enough to permit evacuation of the computer suite before the gas is discharged.

Notes

1. BS 5839: *Fire Detection and Alarm Systems in Buildings*; Part 1: Code of practice for installation and servicing.
2. BS 5445: *Specification for Components of Automatic Fire Detection Systems*; Part 8: High temperature heat detectors.
3. BS 3116: *Automatic Fire Alarm Systems in Buildings*; Part 4: Control and indicating equipment.

Chapter 8

Emergency lighting

A subject closely associated with fire detection and alarm is that of emergency lighting. But it must be remembered that fire is only one of the possible emergencies which, in these violent days, may require the evacuation of a building. Even the failure of the electricity supply can, in certain premises, be sufficient reason for such evacuation. In the event of an emergency of any kind, the occupants of the building should be able to make their escape speedily even when the artificial lighting fails. In fact, emergency lighting should probably more properly be called *escape lighting*, because this is a more accurate description of its function.

The purpose of emergency lighting is to illuminate the escape routes and direction signs on those routes for three purposes:

1. To draw such routes to the immediate attention of occupants of the building who may be unfamiliar with its layout and the location of safe escape routes.
2. To provide sufficient illumination to render the use of those routes speedy and safe.
3. To ensure that fire alarm call points and fire fighting equipment provided along the escape routes can be readily located.

Emergency lighting in the past

One of the boom businesses in recent years has been the production and installation of emergency lighting. A conservative estimate of the value of this work between the years 1973 and 1980 in the UK has been given as £210 million. As with all boom businesses in which the regulating standards have not been adequately formulated it has, sadly, attracted some fortune hunters with substandard equipment. The problem was that emergency lighting was unknown in most buildings in the immediate post-war years, except for places of public entertainment like theatres, cinemas and dance halls. It required a few disastrous fires in hotels, office buildings and factories in the 1950s and 1960s to awaken the public, and the legislative bodies, to the need for a more general use of emergency lighting, together with general regulating standards and criteria of performance for such systems.

Even the *Factories (Standards of Lighting) Regulations 1941* only concerned itself with normal lighting levels – many of which were so low as to be more appropriate to today's emergency illumination levels. Similarly, the *Offices, Shops and Railway Premises Act 1963* made no reference to emergency lighting.

It was not until 1969 that the first important publication dealing with the subject made its appearance. This was a booklet entitled *Recommendations for the Provision of Emergency Lighting in Premises* and was published by the Association of Manufacturers Allied to the Electrical and Electronics Industry. This acted as a spur to the industry to start to think seriously about emergency lighting.

A number of developments had completely changed the character of emergency lighting since the immediate post-war years. In those days, before the transistor and the dry, non-vented alkaline cell battery, emergency lighting was a cumbersome business, involving central battery systems using massive lead-acid single cells positioned in battery rooms which, many said, themselves constituted a considerable fire risk. In fact, many building owners preferred their exit signs to be powered by gas. Now, in the 1970s, the way was open for the design of compact, stand-alone emergency luminaires with integral chargers.

The *Fire Precautions Act* in 1971 did not actually contain the words 'emergency lighting', although a small section says that 'the means of egress must be capable of use at all material times' and implies the need for illumination during the hours of darkness. A Designating Order made under this Act, SI 1972 No 238 recommended the installation of escape lighting in hotels and boarding houses, covering stairways, escape routes and direction and exit signs. The *Health and Safety at Work Act 1974* implied that if employees could be on the premises during the hours of darkness, or be in areas without daylight, emergency lighting was needed. Enforcement for such lighting rested with local fire inspectors who had no firm criteria on which to base their judgements.

Such criteria were eventually provided by BS 5266: Part 1: 1975[1], which concerned the emergency lighting of buildings other than cinemas and certain other specified premises used for entertainment. This document, too, was not without shortcomings. It has been argued that its minimum lux levels are too low, that the one-hour duration batteries which it permits in certain circumstances are too limited, and that the 5-second delay which it also permits before the emergency lights come on is too long. The industry itself has, however, done much to remove the existing doubts and confusion. The Industry Committee for Emergency Lighting (ICEL) has produced a valuable standard for construction and performance of emergency luminaires (ICEL 1001) and an Applications Guide (ICEL 1003)[2].

Other legislation which applies includes the *Cinematograph Act 1972*, the *Theatre Act 1968*, the *Private Places of Entertainment (Licensing) Act 1967* and the *Gaming Act 1968*. Many authorities have published their own recommendations, such as the Greater London Council, the Lancashire County Council and the City of Manchester Council.

Types of emergency lighting

There are three types of emergency lighting:

Escape lighting This is required to illuminate the escape routes effectively at all material times (when the building is occupied) to a minimum level (see later) even under the most inclement conditions; i.e. when the batteries are at the end of their rated life, at the effective minimum lamp output, at the end of the required duration period and without the benefit of inter-reflections from walls and ceilings being considered.

Safety lighting This is intended to ensure the safety of persons involved in potentially hazardous processes in the event of a failure of the normal lighting. This aspect is not specifically covered in BS 5266.

Standby lighting This involves the supply of sufficient illuminance to allow normal activities or processes to continue on failure of the normal lighting. It implies considerable importance or danger attaching to these tasks; e.g. hazardous production processes, or ones that would become hazardous if interrupted, hospital operating theatres etc.

Systems and equipment

There are three systems of emergency lighting using different equipment:

1. *Systems using self-contained (single-point) luminaires* The luminaires in this case contain all the elements required for the system: battery, lamp, control unit and test and monitoring facilities (Fig. 8.1). All that is needed is for the luminaire to be connected to a convenient unswitched mains supply. This ensures that the rechargeable battery is on charge while the mains voltage is available, the luminaire automatically switching to battery operation on the failure of the supply.

    These systems are quick and easy to install and provide a cost-effective and adaptable method, particularly for the small building. No maintenance is required and local supply to luminaires gives automatic monitoring of each sub-circuit. Disadvantages include: a shorter battery life (sealed nickel-cadmium cells can have claimed lives between 5 and 7 years; sealed lead-acid maintenance free cells between 4 and 5 years) when compared with the vented batteries used in central systems; unsuitability for use in high ambient temperatures; the luminaires cannot be linked to the fire alarm system so that they are automatically illuminated when an alarm is given; and units cannot be automatically or manually switched off to prevent unnecessary discharge of the battery during periods of mains failure during daylight hours or when the building is unoccupied.

87

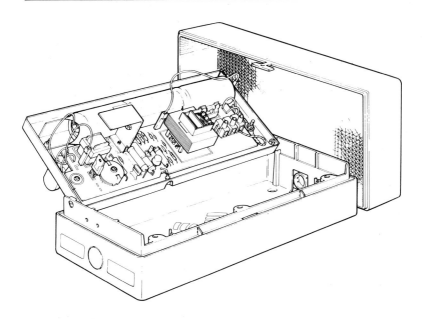

Fig. 8.1 Bardic drawing of single point luminaire

2. *Central battery systems*   These systems consist of a central battery supplying a number of slave luminaires. The battery is normally kept on charge. The supply may be ac or dc and is available either when the normal supply fails or at all material times.

   Advantages of this type of system are: batteries can have a life of up to 25 years; it is a cost-effective solution for larger premises with 40 luminaires or more; the system may be interconnected to the fire alarm system; and most standard luminaires can be used with such a system. The batteries can, of course, be sited in an optimum operating environment, but larger systems do require well-ventilated battery control rooms. The system will require additional fuse-failure monitors to provide sub-circuit protection and the long cable runs may increase vulnerability of the system to fire and sub-circuit failure.

   The capacity of the battery in ampere hours is established by first deciding upon the number of lighting points and their wattages and then applying the following formula:

$$\frac{\text{no. of points} \times \text{wattage of each} \times \text{duration time required}}{\text{voltage of system}}$$

3. *Central generator systems*   These systems consist of a central generator supplying a number of slave luminaires; but because it is impossible for most generators to start up and be placed on load in the 5 seconds laid down in BS

5266: Part 1 as being the maximum delay before the full operation of the emergency lighting system, these systems often have to contain batteries, capable of running the luminaires for at least one hour. Where the generator is capable of running the system within 5 seconds, it will have to be of the mains-failure automatic-start type. Even when systems have a battery back-up, this type of generator is still recommended. Standby lighting can be supplied by central generator systems and the duration of such standby lighting is only limited by the size of the fuel stocks. A minimum of 12 hours supply should always be held for systems which exclusively run escape lighting.

Central generator systems have a greater load carrying capacity than central battery systems; they do, however, have the environmental disadvantages of noise, heat, smell and the storage of fuel, as well as the need for a special enclosure.

Types of self-contained luminaires

There are four types of self-contained emergency lighting luminaires: the non-maintained luminaire, the maintained luminaire, the sustained luminaire, and the combined luminaire.

Non-maintained luminaires contain one or more lamps which are automatically switched on when the normal electricity supply fails. In other words, they are not lit when the normal supply is available.

Maintained luminaires contain one or more lamps which operate from the normal supply at all times when the normal supply is available. When failure occurs, the lamp (or lamps) is automatically supplied from the batteries. Maintained luminaires are lit at all material times; i.e. when the building is occupied.

Sustained luminaires contain two or more lamps, at least one of which is supplied by the normal electricity supply, the other by the emergency supply. This luminaire sustains illumination at all material times with the emergency lamp(s) being non-maintained.

Combined luminaires make up a group of sustained luminaires, the title having been recently introduced by IEC/BSI. It denotes a sustained luminaire in which the emergency lamps may be non-maintained or maintained.

Self-contained luminaires may take the form of a single-point luminaire containing all the appropriate elements for its operation; a luminaire in the form of an illuminated sign, with lettering size and style complying with BS 5266 (Fig. 8.2); a self-contained projector unit comprising one or more tungsten or tungsten halogen lamps, often mounted remotely from a control box (Fig. 8.3); or a modified mains-voltage luminaire which has been converted into a maintained or sustained emergency luminaire using a conversion kit (Fig. 8.4).

Fig. 8.2 Exit luminaire

Fig. 8.3 A Menvier projector unit

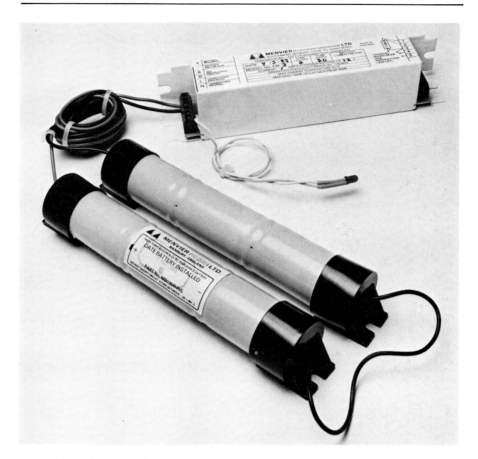

Fig. 8.4 Menvier conversion unit

In the case of the simple single-point luminaire, although the majority are single-unit fittings, in a few cases some components can be mounted separately subject to a maximum separation distance of 500 mm. For instance, the lamps and control gear could be inside the luminaire and the battery outside, or in the case of a lift car, the luminaire can be inside the car and the control gear outside on its roof (Fig. 8.5).

Particular care must be exercised in the use of modification units. While the form is clearly most useful when converting existing installations, refitting existing premises or where the number of light fittings on a ceiling is being carefully controlled for aesthetic reasons, attention needs to be given to the electrical, mechanical and photometric performance of the modified luminaires. In the case of purpose-built self-contained luminaires, their performance is predetermined. This is not the case of a converted unit. In addition to the need to check its emergency lighting performance, its mains-voltage operation after conversion must be checked also to make sure that this has not been impaired. Care too must be taken to ensure

91

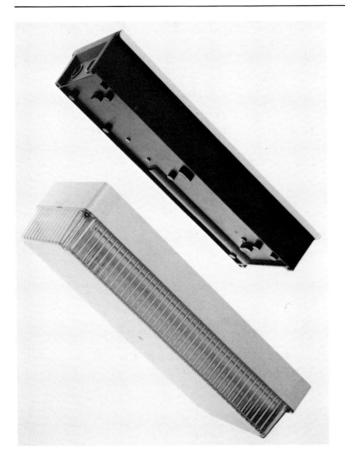

Fig. 8.5 Lift emergency light in two sections

that the added components, such as the sealed batteries, are fitted in surroundings that will not degrade their performance.

While modification units have an important part to play, particularly where high lumen outputs are needed (in large open areas or where standby lighting is required), in less than expert hands they can cause a problem. Preferably only approved organisations should be employed to carry out the modifications – ideally the original manufacturer of the mains-voltage luminaire.

A few points should be remembered when considering the expected life of rechargeable batteries in single-point luminaires. Both the sealed nickel cadmium and the sealed lead-acid cells used can have their lives considerably shortened if three events occur:

1. A continuous high charging current will cause the cells to 'gas' and lose electrolyte which cannot be replaced.
2. If emergency duration is longer than that for which the unit is designed and if the unit is not fitted with a deep discharge protection device, the cell will

continue to discharge for as long as it is able. This deep discharge can reduce battery life in extreme circumstances.

3. If the luminaire has not been designed to dissipate the heat generated during battery charging, this will have a similar effect to high charging.

The construction and operation standards for battery-operated emergency lighting equipment are set down in ICEL: 1001: 1978 which was originally published by the Industry Committee for Emergency Lighting to complement BS 5266: Part 1: 1975. Since then the International Electrotechnical Commission (IEC) has published a section on emergency lighting – IEC 598 – which has been adopted by the BSI as BS 4533: 102.22. This and the ICEL Industrial Standard now bear a close similarity.

ICEL has developed a Certification Scheme covering all types of emergency luminaires, using the independent testing and certification services of the BSI.

Self-powered signs

Illuminated signs which require no battery or wiring are available. They are powered by an integral radioactive source. They are slim and easy to fit, but because of their low level of light emission, they cannot be considered as contributing to the emergency lighting scheme. They are covered by BS 4218 and special precautions will be necessary when disposing of the radioactive material.

Designing the emergency lighting scheme

Guidelines to be followed when planning an emergency lighting scheme in most non-recreational premises, other than private houses, are contained in BS 5266: Part 1. These consist of the following factors:

1. The lighting levels on the escape routes.
2. The duration of the lighting.
3. The layout of the emergency luminaires.

Lighting levels on the escape routes

BS 5266 lays down a minimum floor-level horizontal illuminance on the centre-line of the escape route of 0.2 lux with a uniformity ratio better than 40:1. This minimum is established after allowance has been made for a series of factors which will decrease the output of the luminaires; such factors as reduced battery voltage at the end of its duration and at the end of its declared life, variations in control gear performance, temperature, deterioration due to the age of the luminaires and accumulations of dust on the light controlling surfaces of the luminaires. It therefore follows that the initial performance of the installation will have to give an illuminance considerably in excess of 0.2 lux.

It has been suggested that 0.2 lux is not a satisfactory minimum level in some situations. For instance, while it is adequate for straightforward, uncluttered and level escape routes, it may prove inadequate in factories and supermarkets where escape routes can become obstructed. Similarly, higher levels will be necessary where old people are involved (old persons' homes and geriatric units). Some engineers have suggested considerable increases in illuminance levels in industrial locations where there are hot furnaces or machines which will continue to operate during the light failure. Here they talk in terms of 1.0 lux or 1% of the normal illuminance, whichever is greater. They also suggest a level as high as 5.0 lux or 5% of the normal illuminance on difficult, uneven escape routes, likely to be used by people unfamiliar with the route, or where there are other potential dangers. Critics of BS 5266 point out that dense smoke can quickly render emergency lighting ineffective, particularly when the lights are fixed at high level. They make a plea for emergency lights at low level which will remain visible when the building fills up with smoke down to about 0.5 m or so. In some buildings this requirement could introduce a danger of accidental damage or vandalism.

As any increase in lighting levels means a proportional increase in the amount of power required by the system, ICEL: 1003 suggests the coupling of 3-hour duration luminaires on the escape routes with 1-hour duration luminaires in associated work areas which are likely to be quickly evacuated. This type of planning decision can only be taken after consultation with the local enforcement authority.

Duration of the lighting

Emergency lighting should be maintained for periods varying from 1 to 3 hours (see Table 8.1). Once more some engineers are critical of the inclusion of 1-hour luminaires in multi-storey dwellings up to 10 storeys high. They point out the impossibility in the time to evacuate the building, call the roll, go back and search for an injured person and, perhaps, have to await the arrival of an ambulance before evacuating the injured person.

Layout of emergency luminaires

The layout of emergency lighting luminaires should be determined at an early planning stage taking into account factors already implied in the previous section dealing with illuminance levels and uniformity ratio on escape routes. Various other recommendations are made in BS 5266.

Luminaires and signs should be so sited as to indicate clearly the exit routes and the final exits from the premises. The areas outside final exits should be lit to at least the same level as the area immediately inside the exit so that people using the escape route can move away from it to areas of safety. Particular hazards on an escape route should be illuminated. This means that emergency luminaires should be positioned at intersections of corridors, near changes of direction in the route and near each staircase or flight of steps so that each flight receives direct light (Fig. 8.6).

Table 8.1 Recommended emergency lighting systems

Types of premises	Mode of emergency luminaire	Duration (hrs)
Residential hotels, clubs, schools, hospitals, nursing homes	Maintained or non-maintained	3
Small premises as above, with not more than 10 bedrooms and not more than one floor above or below ground	Maintained or non-maintained	1
Licensed theatres, concert halls, public houses, restaurants	Maintained	2
Unlicensed theatres, concert halls, restaurants	Maintained or non-maintained	2
Libraries, offices, shops	Non-maintained	1
Multi-storey dwellings up to 10 storeys	Non-maintained	1
Multi-storey dwellings above 10 storeys	Non-maintained	3

(Derived from the recommendations contained in BS 5266: Part 1)

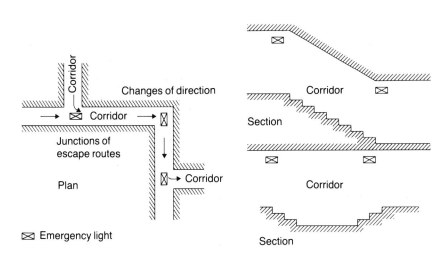

Fig. 8.6 Diagram showing the positioning of emergency lights

Emergency luminaires should also be placed to illuminate all alarm call points and fire fighting equipment. Lift cars, and rooms containing plant, controls or switchgear should be fitted with emergency luminaires; also toilets and cloakrooms exceeding 8m² in area should be similarly covered.

It is important to remember that the local authority and fire prevention departments may have their own recommendations which could override the recommendations of BS 5266. Early consultation with these bodies is essential. Without a fire certificate signed by the local fire officer, the building cannot be occupied.

Maintenance

Emergency lighting systems should be regularly maintained and a record should be kept of each routine examination and test. Regular maintenance should include such items as:

(a) the cleaning of signs and luminaires;
(b) the cleaning of battery terminals;
(c) where applicable, the battery electrolyte should be topped up and terminals greased;
(d) generators and their associated starting equipment should be checked and cleaned, fuel stocks assessed against the specified running time and the oil level in the sump checked;
(e) air intakes and exhausts must be free from obstructions;
(f) particular attention should be paid to the need to replace batteries or lamps having regard to their manufacturers' recommendations.

Emergency lighting in places of public entertainment

Special regulations have always applied to this type of accommodation with regard to means of escape and its lighting in the event of an emergency. At the time of writing, recommendations are under review, with discussions taking place in the Home Office Standing Advisory Committee on the Cinematograph (Safety) Regulations regarding cinemas in particular. Also some authorites like the GLC and Manchester Corporation have their own regulations. Local consultation in each case is advised.

General recommendations for emergency lighting in other premises

Table 8.2 summarises the recommendations contained in ICEL: 1003 with regard to emergency lighting systems in buildings of various types.

The following points apply to the general advice given in Table 8.2.

1. The choice of luminaire and mounting height are closely related. Luminaires with high brightness (floodlights and large fluorescent luminaires) will need to be mounted at high level to avoid glare and to obtain the maximum spacing within the 40:1 uniformity ratio recommended in BS 5266. There is a danger, however, of them becoming obscured by smoke. Lower brightness luminaires should be set between 2.0 and 2.5 m above the floor level in most circumstances (2.5 to 3 m in shops and public meeting places). There is a case, as mentioned earlier, for considering low level emergency lights in some premises.
2. Where large open areas are involved (warehouses, industrial premises, covered shopping precincts, etc.) the use of projector-type luminaires is often preferred. Care should be taken to avoid glare, and they should not be positioned in the apex of roofs where they will be quickly obscured by smoke. In industrial premises, mounting heights which are too low can lead to damage by fork lift trucks.

    A sort of street lighting treatment can be used on escape routes as an alternative solution. In this case luminaires should be positioned at 2.5 to 3.0 m above floor level.
3. Where maintained luminaires are used, longer life lamps should be chosen, such as hot or cold cathode fluorescents.
4. In kitchen areas totally enclosed luminaires should be chosen which can be easily kept clean and will not be affected by steam and high temperatures. The same comment will apply to some industrial premises.
5. In sports buildings and gymnasia, wire guards protecting the luminaires or impact-resistant fittings are recommended.
6. In lifts the luminaires should be of the vandal-resistant type. BS 5655 recommends that each luminaire should have two lamps in parallel, if they are of the filament type.

Table 8.2 ICEL recommendations for emergency lighting

Type of premises	Lighting level on escape route (lux)	Additional recommendations	Duration (hrs)	Remarks
Hotels/boarding houses	0.2	0.4 lux at changes of direction, in dining halls, public areas and kitchen working areas	3	2 or even 1 hour permitted by BS for small premises
Offices	0.2	0.4 lux on routes where obstacles can be anticipated	1	Except when associated with higher risk premises
Warehouses and general industrial	0.2	Higher levels recommended in dangerous areas	1	Projector fittings more appropriate in large areas
Hospitals	Grade a: as normal lighting Grade b: one third to one half normal (Hospital Technical memorandum no. 11)		Nursing homes 3 Hospitals – s/b generator	
Schools and colleges	0.2	0.4 in workshops and kitchens	1 (day school) 3 (boarding)	
Shops	0.2	0.4 where obstructions likely	1	Extra lighting at cash points
Meeting halls	0.2 (whole area)	—	1	
Multi-unit dwellings	0.2	—	1 3	Up to 10 storeys 10 storeys and over
Shopping precincts	0.2	General areas have to be well lit to allow free movement	1 to BS 5266 2–3 better	Projector fittings may be better

7. Generally, internally illuminated directional signs are preferable to externally lit signs.
8. Clearly the conditions applying in hospitals and similar institutions are markedly affected by the type of occupant in the particular building and this should be borne in mind when designing the emergency lighting system. Patients may be confined to bed, or wheelchairs, may be using walking frames or be blind or deaf.

Security lighting

Finally, emergency lighting should not be confused with security lighting. Security lighting is employed primarily as a deterrent to the potential wrongdoer or in order to aid surveillance of an area which is the likely scene of a crime attempt. This subject is dealt with in Chapter 11.

Notes

1. BS 5266; Part 1; 1975, *The Emergency Lighting of Premises.*
2. ICEL: 1003: 1982, *Emergency Lighting Applications Guide,* Industry Committee for Emergency Lighting Ltd.

Chapter 9

Pilferage and shoplifting control

The majority of pilferage and shoplifting is fairly petty in nature – small items of limited value pocketed on impulse. There are obvious exceptions to this generalisation – examples in which two or three people (or even large gangs) co-operate in an organised manner to steal substantial amounts of merchandise from shops. These exceptional cases will be touched upon later in this chapter.

Petty theft can occur anywhere; but nowhere more frequently than in shops. Other favourite locations of pilferage are the building site (dealt with in detail in Chapter 13) and places of work. The shopkeeper and employer, like the taxman, seem fair game when it comes to the petty criminal. In fact, the perpetrator of most acts of petty theft does not usually consider himself (or herself) a real criminal, or the act he or she is committing an act of theft. The larger the organisation from which the theft is made, the less these people relate their actions to those of criminals. Even the words society uses to descibe the activity tend to minimise the apparent seriousness of the crime – *shoplifting* sounds better and more socially acceptable than *theft from a shop*; *shrinkage* better than *theft by shop employees*; *fiddling* the taxman better than *fraud*.

The problem is one of kindling the social conscience, more than designing buildings in such a way as to discourage the petty theft. The common factor in all crimes of pilfering is opportunity. Without the opportunity presented by the merchandise laid out on display, or the tools and materials lying around at work, there would usually be no crime. It is rarely a crime provoked by need. But opportunity and the enticement of close display is in-built into so much of our selling techniques today, and as a result the retail store becomes the focus of a massive amount of pilferage.

Just look at a few of the facts. In 1982 the Home Office statistics recorded 242,300 offences of shoplifting in England and Wales; probably this represented only the visible tip of the iceberg of total theft at that time, with substantial numbers of offences going undetected. It has been estimated that thefts from British shops total about £1,000 million per year. In London's Oxford Street stores alone the annual loss through shoplifting (customer pilferage) or shrinkage (staff pilferage) is set at about £50 million. This scale of loss is tackled by the store owners with varying degrees of energy. Generally speaking the greater part of the effort seems to be directed towards reducing customer pilferage. However, some members of the retail industry believe that their losses are greater from thefts by staff, either directly or in collusion with customers, than from unassisted shoplifting by customers. Also smaller businesses seem to be less security conscious than larger national organisations. Some put their faith in store security officers (plain-clothes or uniformed), others in surveillance devices – often more for their deterrent effect than for their success in aiding the apprehending of criminals.

Working party report

In 1973 the Home Office published a report, entitled *Shoplifting, and Thefts by Shop Staff*, which contained the recommendations of the drafting working party on ways in which these crimes could be reduced. While the majority of them concerned management matters, involving the proper training of staff, the institution of adequate stock control methods, the implementation of effective till disciplines including the giving of receipts and the wrapping of goods; some concerned the layout of the stores.

For instance, the report suggested that the local police crime prevention officer should be consulted about the way the merchandise was displayed in the store and the siting of display fittings. His views, the report pointed out, are always valuable on the vulnerability of the goods to opportunist theft.

Store layout, it was suggested, should be arranged so that the displays did not impede the observation of the selling area. Blind corners should be avoided and all parts of the sales area should be observable, if not by direct vision, at least by the use of convex mirrors. In supermarkets and self-service stores, consideration should be given to the use of distinctive price tags, maybe of the electronic type which will excite an alarm if the goods are removed from the shop with the tag in position. Also in this type of store, recommendations were made that the administration offices should be sited to overlook the shopping area – and more specifically the check-out area. The provision of a parking area for customers' bags was also suggested, although this recommendation did not find general approval from shopkeepers.

In 1983 the Home Office again looked at the problem – its findings being contained in a report of the same title as the previous report[1]. It based its conclusions on a limited examination, in two areas of England, of the extent to which the 1973 recommendations had been implemented.

The 1973 report had suggested that firms should consider employing uniformed or plain-clothes security officers and 'technical aids for deterring and detecting shoplifters'. It also said that 'notices advising customers of their use should be prominently displayed'. The findings 10 years later were enlightening.

Of the 91 shops examined in Northumbria; 37 had no security officers or devices, 19 had both, 32 had devices only and 3 had security officers only. In Greater Manchester the sample of 107 premises contained 32 without security personnel or equipment, and of the rest, 54 had security staff, 30 had cctv, 41 had mirrors, eight had loop alarms and 4 had magnetic tags. It is interesting to note that the group of shops which were totally devoid of security provisions included jewellers, radio and TV dealers, clothing shops and food stores.

Opportunity

In Home Office Research Study No 34, *Crime as Opportunity*[2] the following words were used:

'As should be clear, we would question the idea that there is a floating body of people with anti-social tendencies which must be expressed in crime of whatever kind. On the contrary, we believe that criminal behaviour consists of a number of discrete activities which are heavily influenced by particular situational inducements and by the balance of risks and rewards involved.'

The Study goes on to list the situational inducements that affects opportunist crime.

1. The abundance of goods available that fall into a coveted category.
2. The physical security of such objects.
3. Low levels of surveillance.

These clearly make many present-day shops prime targets for the opportunist thief. Goods are tantalisingly dangled in front of the customers' noses; merchandise is less physically secure in today's department store or self-service shop than it once was in the corner shop; and, as the number of shop assistants per m^2 of sale floor area declines, merchandise is less adequately supervised.

What is more, this type of crime is as much affected by the demand for stealable goods as the abundance of such goods. Certainly goods of more individual value, stolen from a store, are less likely to remain in the possession of the thief, but will be rapidly exchanged for cash. Only the smaller items usually remain in the possession of the thief. The current craze for electronic gadgetry, therefore, places these kinds of goods in an extremely vulnerable category – until, at any rate, some other craze replaces it.

Miniaturisation, too, has made the job of the shoplifter so much more easy. Now, relatively valuable articles can often be easily pocketable.

The Home Office Study concludes that 'physical crime prevention ... may prove considerably cheaper than attempts to alter attitudes and abilities of potential offenders' and goes on to suggest that 'physical crime prevention is not simply a matter of intensive policing and crude security, but that it can, in imaginative and unobtrusive ways, utilise technology and architectural expertise to protect vulnerable property ... '.

In short, the best way to reduce opportunist crime is to make it more difficult to commit. While there are architectural ways to reduce opportunist burglary as we have seen in Chapter 5, shoplifting comes into a rather different sphere, in which the selling techniques of the shop owner can be said to be almost totally opposed to better security.

Organised theft

'A new and worrying development' has been noted in the 1983 Home Office report on shoplifting[1] that of 'an increasing number of shoplifters who blatantly steal from stores by force and intimidation of staff and customers'. It further notes 'an increase in organised shoplifting and violence by offenders who are caught', although it points out that this characteristic is, at present, a relatively small part of the whole picture. The Oxford Street Association has reported a similar increase in violence in that area of London's West End and provincial high streets and shopping centres have placed much of the blame for increasing harassment of shop staff on large numbers of unemployed teenagers aimlessly milling about shopping precincts. Unhappily this latter phenomenon would seem to be a sign of the times we live in. Rapid recourse to the police by a '999' call seems to be the only counter measure. Also, the Home Office advises more shops to participate in precautionary 'early warning' schemes to alert each other of gangs operating in the area, in a similar way to the warning scheme which seems to operate successfully in many areas of cheque card fraudsters in the vicinity.

How can the designer help?

Because the sales philosophy of the particular store or shop will dominate the layout of the sales areas, the designer will find the amount of assistance he can give severely limited. It would always be a good idea, though, to enlist the help of the local crime prevention officer at the design stage. His advice might have more weight with the shopkeeper than that of the designer.

As far as the sales floor is concerned, surveillance is all important. All parts of the area should be capable of being supervised by the sales staff at their normal stations. Provide wide gangways and generous circulation space to assist observation by staff. Secluded, blind corners should be avoided. If necessary, quarter and hemispherical mirrors should be used to bring all parts of the store into clear vision. Particular areas which should be well supervised (and be seen to be well supervised) are cash points, particularly check-out points in supermarkets, and exits. The planning of administrative offices overlooking such points might be a good idea.

If a cctv surveillance system is installed, it should cover the whole sales area, with particular attention to the special positions mentioned above. It is often the deterrent effect of these systems, more than their actual help in apprehending a shoplifter, which is important. Quite often the monitors of these systems are left unmanned – hardly an effective use of the capital invested in the installation! Therefore the deterrent effect of cctv systems should be heightened by warning notices and the obtrusiveness of the equipment, which should not only be obvious, but should be seen to be working.

In addition, bearing in mind staff theft, supervision, either personal or by means of cameras, needs to extend to storage areas behind the scenes, as well as staff canteens and other facilities.

Fire escapes are always a weakness in sales premises. Means of escape from all points inside the building are obviously necessary and some of these are likely to be in less well policed areas of the shop. If these exits are unsupervised, they need to be covered by an alarm system which is triggered by their illegal use when no emergency exists. Some of these emergency exit alarms are totally self-contained and independent of the main alarm system. They are battery operated and usually contain a warning that illegal use will cause an alarm to sound. Staff can bypass these alarms by the use of a key.

Also alarm systems may need to be extended to particular goods on display, especially if they are of greater value and are within easy reach of the customers. A single wire can be passed through handles or other enclosed projections on especially valuable articles to form a complete loop to an alarm control box. The loop can be broken at intervals along its length by small in-line plugs and sockets. The assistant throws a bypass switch, situated behind the counter or in some other secure position, then removes the article required from the wire without unthreading the other articles.

These systems are not usually connected to the main alarm system. If they were, a relatively minor incident could disrupt the whole operation of the store. Pressure mats placed under heavier goods provide another localised alarm source, as also do microswitches beneath loaded display shelves.

Security tags can be fixed to the goods and removed at the payment counter. If an attempt is made to leave the shop with the tag still in position, an alarm is raised. Security tags come in two types: passive and active. The passive tags do not transmit a signal, but disturb a very high frequency signal sent out by a sensor unit at the point of exit. There are, however, ways of screening the tags so that the alarm is not set off. Active tags transmit their own signal which is received by the sensor. This means they have to contain a miniature battery, making them somewhat large and expensive. A new form of active tag has been introduced by Securitag (UK). In this the signal transmitted by the sensor unit is split by the tag, then transmitted back to the sensor; the power needed for the tag to transmit being drawn from the original signal.

Such technical aids should be the subject of prominent notices advising the public of their use. The use of store detectives should similarly be advertised.

Personal attack

This appears to be an increasing hazard for staff dealing with money or valuables. It is therefore wise to install an alarm button in some easily accessible, but discreet, place close to the workstation. A foot switch is often used. The alarm switch or button should be self-latching unless the control unit has electronic latching. This means that the alarm will continue, even when pressure on the switch is removed, and the system will need to be reset with a key.

Whether an audible alarm should be sounded, or whether a silent alarm in some other part of the building is more advisable, will depend on the particular circumstances. An audible alarm might put the person under threat at even greater risk.

Store philosophy

Shoplifting is probably the most difficult crime to control by the design of the building. It would be easy enough to design a store whose very character defeated both the opportunist and the gang thief; but such a store would not encourage the bona fide shopper. When the retail trade embarked on the form of free display practised today, it took a calculated gamble, believing its encouragement of greater sales would outweigh the greater losses from shoplifting. Now, being firmly set on this course, there seems to be no going back, and the cost of pilferage has to be minimised in the best way possible. The problem ranges in scale from the well-organised gang, working its way down Oxford Street or Knightsbridge, to the corner sweet shop being turned over by a besieging horde of school children during the lunchtime break, and the one-off sneak thief who gives way to a sudden impulse.

As the Home Office puts it[2]: 'prevention should be based on specifically-directed measures which, by making crime more difficult to commit, discourage the opportunist offender and deter the professional by increasing his chance of being apprehended'.

Notes

1. Review by the Home Office Standing Committee on Crime Prevention 1983; *Shoplifting, and Thefts by Shop Staff*; HMSO 1983.
2. Home Office Research Study No 34; *Crime as Opportunity*; HMSO 1976.

Chapter 10

Integrated security systems

Most existing commercial and industrial premises of any size will already be equipped with some form of fire alarm system, but few older properties have any form of security system other than locks on the doors; or if they do, it will usually be one that is unlikely to be a defence against today's criminal, whose skill seems to increase day by day in response to the sophistication of the defences that confront him.

The idea of high levels of security in ordinary buildings is a relatively new one. And this means that most older installations are a jumble of independent systems which have been tacked onto the building at different times. It is only recently that the idea of integrating all these necessary services of a building into one system has arisen. Take for instance the simple fire alarm system.

Many of the old systems, particularly in smaller properties, consist of a series of manual alarm points activating bells or other forms of sounder. These systems clearly depend for their operation on human initiation and we have already seen, in Chapter 7, that the human alarm often needs to be supplemented by automatic aids, such as fire detectors.

But the fire alarm installation does not necessarily end there. We mentioned, in Chapter 7, installations at the Queensway Centre in Peterborough and the Cape Hill brewery in the West Midlands where other functions were added on to the alarm system, such as the control of automatic fire fighting equipment.

Most new commercial and industrial buildings will need by law to be equipped with at least an efficient fire alarm system and adequate emergency lighting. In addition, most will require some other form of security service – intruder protection, access controls or surveillance systems. Equally, existing buildings, as they are modified or refurbished will also need to be brought into line with current standards of fire and security protection.

 We have noted already that intruder alarm systems, as far as their individual components are concerned, are not dissimilar to fire alarm systems. With the scope offered by the microprocessor, it is quite simple to link these two functions under one central control. What is more, it is not even necessary to stop there. Access control is a related function, using very similar hardware. In fact, many day-to-day management functions of the large commercial or industrial building or group of buildings can be controlled, monitored, and data concerning its operation recorded

106

by merely extending the same electronic control system. The complex heating, lighting and air conditioning services of a building can be controlled and monitored within the same integrated system, giving continuous data on energy usage and plant efficiency. All these functions can, of course, have their own control systems, but there are many advantages in having the whole control operation within one system.

There are many such integrated systems on the market, with major modifications and totally new systems being introduced regularly. It would, therefore, be pointless to discuss these in too much detail. Such discussion would quickly be out of date. In the appendix will be found a list of some of the major manufacturers who offer a comprehensive design service for this type of installation and who would be pleased to discuss any particular project. As far as this book is concerned, it has been decided merely to give an overview of the subject by taking three examples of very different integrated systems, which are on the market at the time of writing, and examining each in some detail.

Henderson Security Systems

Like many other systems on the market, this one developed from a sophisticated access control system. It is able to provide control and monitoring from centralised points, enabling predefined automatic or manual action to be taken against any unauthorised act throughout the premises.

The system can be tailored to the needs of the particular premises, but is founded on the use of modern microprocessor based central control consoles from which the various aspects of security can be monitored and recorded. Revised parameters, too, can be fed into the system from this central control, when the need arises.

The system contains the following basic functions:

Access control

The control of the movement of people around the establishment, including the restriction of access to certain high-security areas according to the status of the employee or the time of day. The system gives a minute-by-minute knowledge of where the personnel are in the building or group of buildings; an essential if lives are to be saved in the event of a disaster.

Alarm systems

The alarm systems are automatically activated in the event of a breach of the security parameters and a chronological log of the events is registered.

extensions – further work

Closed-circuit television

This provides the visual follow-up of any alarm and allows routine surveillance of critical areas with cameras located at strategic points and operated on an automatic or manual mode.

Perimeter protection

A system which detects and analyses any movement of the perimeter fence can be the first line of defence against an intruder. In the Henderson system the perimeter is split into zones, which allows the intrusion area to be instantly identified, when the alarm is signalled, and a swift response mounted.

Vehicle parking

A range of gates, barriers or rising steps, manually or automatically operated, can be installed to protect the parking areas. Access and exit to these areas is automatically held on record.

Time recording

Employee movements entering and leaving the premises can be recorded to give necessary management data for preparing payroll information and to control flexible working hours.

   The benefit of a system such as this is that it provides maximum security for minimum cost. It helps to reduce the risk of theft and vandalism, as well as reducing the costs normally associated with security guards.

Group 4 System 3000

This is another integrated system which has grown out of an entry control facility. It is, therefore, not surprising to find a card access control system at the heart of System 3000. Other facilities which can be tacked on include the monitoring of alarms, shop floor job monitoring and the recording of employee purchases etc. This is a two-level system, the second level providing more sophisticated supervisory and administrative facilities. Not only logging, but reporting facilities are possible with direct data communication with other non-security computers.

key words

AFA-Minerva System 4000

The basis of this extremely comprehensive system is the System 4100 Multizone Fire Controller and Multizone Security Controller. Both facets of this are capable of providing protection for large buildings requiring complex plant or event

108

Fig. 10.1 Group 4 System 3000 level one or level two controllers. Programmed data can also be entered into the level one controller by a hand programmer

programming and a combination of security zones and door monitoring zones. It can monitor a large number of fire detectors and call points or intruder alarms and all fire and security zones can be individually isolated.

The System 4000 is a modular package. Onto the fire and security modules above can be added a selection of additional modules to suit the particular requirements of the premises. These all add up to a totally comprehensive control and management package. Additional facilities include:

System 4200 surveillance equipment

Up to 8 cctv cameras can be connected to each System 4200 with cameras and lenses for any application, indoors or out.

System 4300 flexible microcomputer

This monitors events and controls other system functions, storing events with time and date on floppy disk and producing hard print-out as required.

109

System 4400 card access control

This is a flexible on-line access system, using the patented Thorn EMI Watermark Card. The system has a card memory capacity of up to 20,000 individual codes.

System 4500 multidata transmission system

This is used where hardwiring to a central controller is too costly. Fire, security, plant or any other event signal can be transmitted via the multiplexing system on a two-wire transmission link.

System 4600 mini-computer system

This is intended for use in large installations where a high degree of multi-tasking or event monitoring and control is required.

System 4700 watchman's patrol monitor

Clocking points are established at strategic intervals around a site or within a building to enable any effective sequenced patrol to be programmed. Departures from the programmed sequence or timing causes the alarm to be raised.

System 4800 building management and energy control system (BMEC 4800)

Unlike many conventional building automation systems which only monitor building activity and energy consumption, the BMEC 4800 offers a completely integrated system for direct control, supervision and operation automatically. Facilities offered by the system include:

(a) fixed time start/stop control;
(b) optimum start/stop control;
(c) maximum demand monitoring;
(d) load cycling and shedding;
(e) temperature setpoint control;
(f) outside temperature compensation;
(g) boiler sequencing;
(h) meter monitoring;
(i) manual start/stop;
(j) change of state reporting and control;
(k) lighting control.

System 4950 public address

A PA system can prove a useful security aid. It can be used to control emergency situations by concise live or prerecorded instructions, warning personnel of potentially dangerous conditions when normally safe escape routes could prove hazardous, communicating with personnel involved in an emergency (e.g. trapped in a lift), as well as a variety of non-security communication uses.

More than a security system

It must be clear from the above that integrated systems have led us out of the realm of the simple security system into the field of total building management. Such systems are capable of undertaking a range of tasks which can be summarised as follows:

- protection of losses from fire by alarm and automatic extinguishing,
- protection against theft or the damage of property by intruders,
- monitoring, control and recording of personnel movement,
- effective utilisation of energy in heating, lighting and air conditioning,
- planned maintenance of engineering services equipment and internal communication.

Chapter 11

External security and security lighting

The external perimeter of the site represents the first line of defence in any security system, but it is a defence which is rarely used (or even appropriate) in the majority of buildings. For instance, it is a rather unusual private house which is surrounded by a security fence, although the majority are surrounded by a fence or hedge which demarcates the boundary of the site and is, therefore, an indication of ownership rather than a security barrier. Equally the high street store's external security is usually restricted to walls round the service yard at the back, a gate and one or two security lights.

This, in fact, indicates quite neatly the extent of the average need for external security. Generally buildings rely on the impenetrability of their external shells to deter intrusion. Only when buildings are in the special security risk category, situated in remote locations or surrounded by unsupervised space or storage areas are security fences generally needed. In fact a security perimeter can even be helpful to a criminal. Once inside the perimeter, he is screened from the outside world and only has the eyes of any resident or visiting security guards to worry about. Here, in relative seclusion, he can plan the next stage of his penetration into the building without too much risk of being observed.

Also, it would be neither architecturally desirable nor economically sensible to surround buildings with security fencing and other forms of discouragement to entrance, if these were not strictly necessary. In many respects we come back once more to the question of defensible space, discussed in Chapter 3. Generally, only when the spaces around buildings are unsupervised and not overlooked is there usually a need for external security barriers.

The elements of external security

External security equipment falls broadly into three major categories; fences, gates and lighting. This equipment can also be supplemented by intruder alarms in some cases and, in the case of buildings with particular security problems, by cctv camera coverage.

As with other types of security, the degree of the threat to a building needs to be assessed before the type of external defences can be selected. Once more these fall into the familiar classifications: opportunist entry and deliberate intrusion.

The most likely threat is from opportunist entry. In this case the culprit is encouraged to enter the site through curiosity and because the entry appears to be easy. He will not be carrying breaching aids of any description to help him over difficult barriers and fences and he probably will not even attempt to force entry into the building, once inside the perimeter, unless some obvious means of entry suggests itself. This criminal is looking for what he can find lying around and is anxious not to encounter difficulties. Immediately the going gets rough, he is off to new pastures. He may well, however, resort to a little vandalism on the way, which can be very costly to the building owner. A fence that is only moderately difficult to climb is usually sufficient to put off this type of criminal.

Opportunist entry is by far the most common form of external intrusion, and the most easy to deter. Deliberate intrusion, however, is another matter. This involves premeditation and a certain amount of preplanning. In this type of entry the criminal is likely to approach the job with some degree of preparedness. He may well arrive with breaching aids of some description. He is not acting on impulse; he has come there for the specific purpose of committing a burglary or even an act of terrorism.

Fencing

Opportunist entry will be deterred by a relatively simple chainlink fence, provided it is well maintained and cannot be easily climbed. So often these fences become distorted during their life and entry points, which could be simply avoided if the fence were regularly inspected, begin to appear. Fig. 11.1 shows a relatively simple fence with a little more strength than the average chainlink version. It is manufactured by the Expanded Metal Company and should give good long-term service in keeping out opportunist intruders. Fig. 11.2 shows details of a pallisade type of security fence, manufactured by Hill and Smith, the fixings of which have been designed to give maximum resistance to vandal attack.

Anti-intruder chainlink fencing with cranked top sections is covered by BS 1722: Part 10: 1972. But, in spite of the name, none of these fences is likely to be proof against a determined attack by an intruder with equipment and the time and opportunity to use it.

This type of attack has been examined by the American company, Man Barrier Corporation, who has pointed out that a chainlink fence, surmounted by barbed wire or a barbed wire concertina can be crossed without the help of breaching aids. If a form of General Purpose Barbed Tape Obstacle (GPBTO Type 2) were substituted for the barbed wire, unaided entry would be rendered impossible. The normal chainlink fence with barbed wire, according to Man Barrier, would have to be supplemented by intruder sensors on the fence posts, if a determined intruder were to be kept out.

113

Fig. 11.1 Expanet Universal fence

Given a pair of bolt cutters, Man Barrier points out, a hole could be cut through the chainlink mesh, bypassing the GPBTO on top. This could only be countered by placing additional GPBTO coils on the ground inside the fence – not a very pleasant

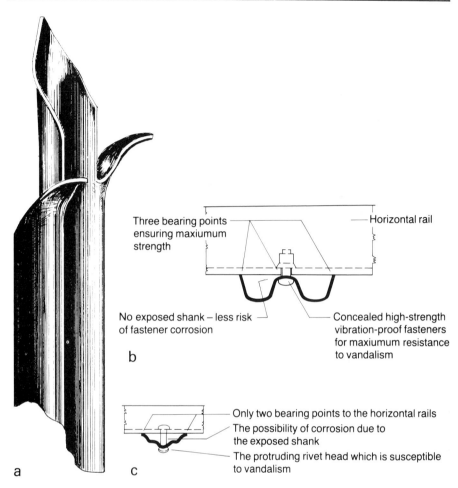

Three bearing points ensuring maxiumum strength

Horizontal rail

No exposed shank – less risk of fastener corrosion

Concealed high-strength vibration-proof fasteners for maxiumum resistance to vandalism

b

Only two bearing points to the horizontal rails

The possibility of corrosion due to the exposed shank

The protruding rivet head which is susceptible to vandalism

a   c

Fig. 11.2 Maximum security fence from Hill and Smiths. (a) Maximum security palisade with triple-pointed head. (b) Fixing detail of palisade. (c) Typical example of the fixing of other types of corrugated palisade

prospect. So once more we are back to intruder detectors, or even guard dogs within the perimeter of the site.

All this suggests that a security fence for the normal building is anything but secure, when attacked by a determined intruder. But this, as we have seen, is a rare occurrence and therefore may not be considered worth considering in thee terms. Certainly the alternative seems somewhat daunting, in Man Barrier terms – a double perimeter fence with additional coils of GPBTO, producing an effect similar to many concentration camp perimeter fences, or its TOPS Total Perimeter Security System – a 1500 mm diameter stainless steel unclimable barrier with a concealed electronic detection and signalling system within the tube formed by the barrier (Fig. 11.3).

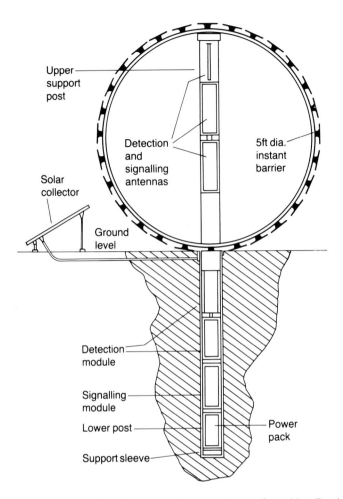

Upper support post

Solar collector

Detection and signalling antennas

5ft dia. instant barrier

Ground level

Detection module

Signalling module

Lower post

Power pack

Support sleeve

Fig. 11.3 Tops Total Perimeter Security System from Man Barrier

Gates

Gates, whether vehicular or pedestrian, fulfil two distinct, but not mutually exclusive, functions. They are used to control and record the movement of vehicles or personnel into and out of the site, or from one part of a site to another; they are also used to prohibit unauthorised entry.

Dealing first with vehicular gates or barriers, these can be successful in prohibiting the entry of vehicles while not restricting pedestrians. The most obvious example of this is the boom barrier (Fig. 11.4), particularly one which is not fitted with skirts. These can be manual or motorised, the latter version being controllable locally or remotely, from a control console, or by key switches, card

116

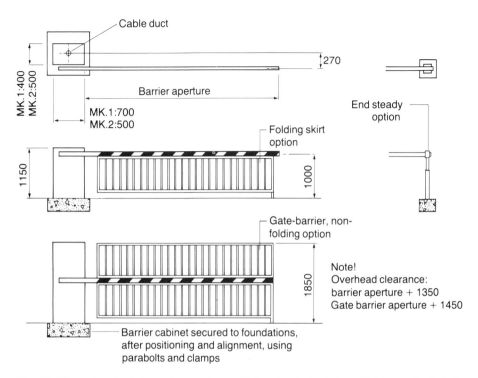

Fig. 11.4 Boom barrier (dimensions are in mm) (drawing derived from Pitts Security Gates' boom barriers)

readers, or vehicle detection loops; in fact any system which produces a signal or operates a contact.

Boom barriers, however, do not prohibit determined vehicular access, assuming a certain amount of noisy destruction is not considered a deterrent. Therefore, particularly in unsupervised locations, it is not unusual to use a rising road barrier in conjunction with a boom barrier. Rising road barriers consist of a steel frame supporting a heavy duty, anti-skid barrier plate. In its retracted position, the plate lies flush with the surrounding road surface, with the supporting frame housed in a pit beneath. In the erect position the plate forms a barrier across the roadway, approximately 350 mm high (Fig. 11.5). The operation is usually by means of an electrohydraulic powerpack, the motor and the pump being mounted remotely for ease of access and maintenance. Control can be by any of the means applicable to operating a boom barrier. It is recommended that rising road barriers should be installed in conjunction with traffic light control to indicate when the barrier is in the lowered position. Usually the driver cannot see the barrier because of the bonnet of his car.

Other forms of motorised gates fall into two main categories: sliding gates and swing gates. Sliding gates are generally considered to have several benefits over swing gates; they do not obstruct a part of the roadway by the opening radii of the

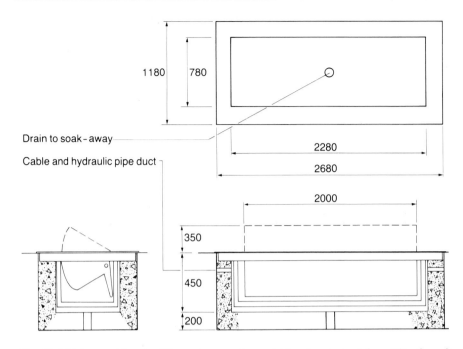

1180   780

Drain to soak-away

Cable and hydraulic pipe duct

2280

2680

2000

350

450

200

Fig. 11.5 Rising road barrier (dimensions are in mm) (drawing derived from Pitts Security Gates' rising road barriers)

leaves and they can generally cope with wider roadways without resort to a two-leaf format. On the other hand, sliding gates do require a substantial run-back area for the gate when open. This will need a length equivalent to the length of the clear aperture of the gate, plus an extra dimension, possibly in the region of 1.5 m. Sliding gates clearly cannot be used where there are flanking walls or other boundaries on either side of the roadway.

It is useful to remember the method of stating the hand of a gate. Firstly, the gate is always considered as though it were being observed from outside (i.e. from the less secure side). The hand of a swing gate is the side on which the hinges are situated; while the hand of a sliding gate is the side of its motor (i.e. the side of the run-back). Some sliding gates work on a cantilever principle, not requiring a floor track or intermediate support across the opening. These are usually driven via a channel on the base of the moving leaf and are supported on a beam which extends on the run-back side of the opening (Fig. 11.6). The maximum width of this type of gate is usually around 12 m.

An alternative cantilever form makes use of a top support. In this case the bottom of the gate can be profiled to match the slope of the roadway across the aperture – a feature that is not possible on the other version. This type of gate is ideal where the site is likely to flood, or be subject to considerable blowing dust or debris (Fig. 11.7). The maximum width of this type of gate is usually around 15 m.

Wider sliding gates, or ones where the gate is very high or heavy, are usually of the

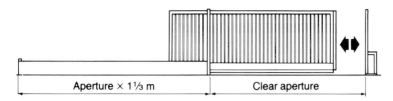

Fig. 11.6 LoTracker gate (Pitts Security Gates)

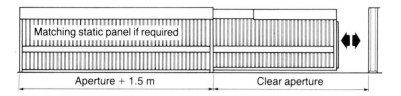

Fig. 11.7 HiTracker gate (Pitts Security Gates)

tracked variety with a floor track grouted into a narrow trench across the full width of the roadway.

The leaf size of hinged motorised gates is usually restricted to about 5 m, giving a normal maximum width of a two leaf gate of about 10 m (Fig. 11.8).

Pedestrian gates can be of the swing, sliding or turnstile type. Hinged gates can be designed to ensure that the gate cannot be inadvertently left open and some gates are fitted with buzzers and lights which operate when the gate is being used.

Control systems for gates can be of a wide variety of types. These vary from the basic pushbutton control, situated near the gate or in some remote location, to complex card entry systems referred to in Chapter 6. In addition, gates can be operated by high-security keyswitches fitted to the gateposts or in a remote control point, or radio controlled by hand-held battery powered transmitters or from a mains powered unit (the signal is coded to provide security), or operated by means of a vehicle detection loop below the road surface. Alternatively, a combination of these systems can be used which is tailored to the particular needs of the organisation.

Also, motorised gates of all types will need certain safety devices to avoid accidents to people and vehicles. These include pneumatically operated safety edges to gates, which halt and reverse their movement on touching an obstruction. Also additional devices are often included, such as cctv remote gate surveillance, flashing lights on the gateleaf which operate during movement, intercom or telephone communication from the gate to a security point and traffic signals.

Security lighting

Darkness is an unfailing friend to the wrongdoer. One of the simplest ways of protecting any space, whether inside or out, is to make it readily visible to the public

Fig. 11.8 Broughton Controls automatic gate

at large. In other words, when the natural light fails, artificial lights take over. A security fence is much more difficult to scale or cut through when it is bathed in light. The criminal is never certain whether he is being observed or not. What is more, light helps to deter criminal acts inside the building, as well as outside. The dimly lit shop on a shopping street is less likely to be broken into than the totally unlit shop, because the former is so much more easily supervised by the general public, or even the patrolling policeman, passing by its windows. Similarly, light can deter the criminal even when there is little danger of the light actually illuminating his activities. For instance, the automatic and random switching on and off of lights in the unoccupied private house can make the would-be burglar believe that someone is at home and encourage him to move on elsewhere. There are a number of time switches on the market which will allow this deception to be undertaken.

In external security, lighting is even more important. It has already been explained that a perimeter fence, once penetrated, can become a protection to the intruder. This illusion of safety is very quickly dispelled if the area inside is illuminated.

Generally, it is wise to give overall lighting to all storage areas surrounding buildings, and all building perimeters in secluded locations or where break-ins are considered likely. A system made up of street lighting units on standards or as wall-mounted fittings and using mercury or sodium vapour lamps is usually most economic and efficient. Where cctv surveillance equipment is at work, security lighting may become a necessity, but this will be discussed in more detail later on.

It is even worth considering the use of some form of external lighting around the normal private residence. This need not cost much to run, particularly if fittings are used which can contain the new breed of miniature fluorescent lamp (Thorn 2D, Phillips PL and the Osram Opus) or the low wattage high pressure sodium lamps (Fig. 11.9). All these light sources use considerably less energy than the equivalent tungsten lamp for the same or better light output and have longer life expectancy.

All external security lighting can be controlled by photoelectric cell switches, if required, to ensure their automatic switching according to the level of daylight. Also, if the limiting of electric consumption is important, security lighting can be linked to radar movement detectors which automatically switch the lights on when a prowler is sensed. These lights have an in-built light-sensing element which avoids continuous operation during daylight.

The element of surprise can always be relied upon to deter the intruder. Mobile alarm units, which detect movement and switch on integral flashing flood lamps and sirens, can be placed to cover particularly vulnerable areas in the perimeter where access might be attempted.

Intruder alarms

Outdoor intruder alarms fall into two categories: microwave and infra-red beam-breaking systems.

The microwave detectors are not of the volumetric type, but the type emitting a narrow beam of radio waves to a receiver up to 152 m away. The microwaves will pass through chainlink fencing and therefore, when protecting a site perimeter, they must be arranged so that external movement does not set off false alarms. The usual method of using these detectors out of doors is to arrange the beam to run parallel to, and just inside, the perimeter fence.

Fig. 11.9 Allekat GTE Sylvania's low wattage security floodlights

Microwaves can be attenuated by rain and fog and units used outside should be equipped with automatic gain controls to compensate for this. Also small objects, such as birds or cats, can trigger off the alarm unless a minimum size restraint is built into the system.

Infra-red radiation detectors have the advantage over microwave devices that they have a longer range (up to 300 m) and also their beams can be reflected by mirrors, allowing one detector to cover a rectangular enclosure, whereas four microwave detector units would be required (see Fig. 11.10).

Reflection of the infra-red beam does, however, reduce its strength and snow or ice can render reflection impossible. In fact, these conditions can attenuate the beam in direct transmitter/receiver situations unless an in-built thermostatically controlled heater is part of the unit. Microwave equipment is much less affected by cold conditions.

Infra-red detectors can also be triggered off by small objects such as birds and cats breaking the beam. In this case two beams, side by side, are required, the alarm being raised only when both beams are broken. This, however, has the disadvantage of doubling the cost of the sensors by doubling the number of projectors and receivers.

Infra-red detector beams 'laced' by mirrors across a gap between buildings is an extremely effective way of detecting unwary prowlers around the outside of buildings (see Fig. 11.11).

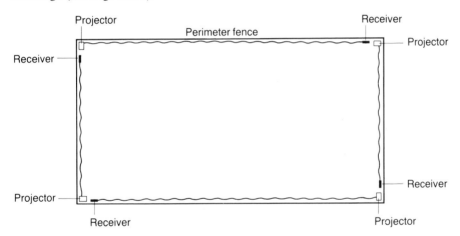

Fig. 11.10 Diagram of perimeter guarded by infra-red and microwave detectors

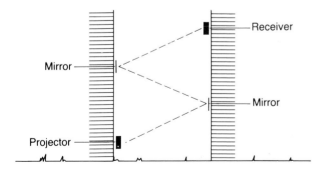

Fig. 11.11 Lacing infra-red detector beams between buildings

Closed-circuit television

This form of surveillance is clearly not a wholly external phenomenon. Probably the most common use of cctv security is in retail premises. However, it is becoming more frequently used today in office and industrial security, sometimes internally, covering particular areas of extreme security risk, sometimes externally to cover entrances to the building or to the site.

Cctv is frequently used to monitor access points and it has the advantage of providing remote surveillance and allowing visitors and others to be screened and observed from a position of safety. A video recorder can, of course, be attached to the system and the recordings so made can be used as evidence in court should the need arise.

Cameras can be concealed, or can be mounted obtrusively to act as a deterrent to the criminal. They can be of the fixed type, or they can be controlled remotely from the monitor station; panning and tilting to survey the whole area, and zooming in on suspicious movements. In its simplest form the system can consist of a series of cameras, each connected to a monitor. Alternatively, more than one camera can be connected to each monitor, in which case it becomes the responsibility of the security officer to switch regularly from camera to camera to obtain a complete picture of the security of his premises. Some installations have automatic sequential switching from camera to camera to avoid laziness of operation. The timing of the switching is usually adjustable from 2 to 30 seconds.

An important factor to appreciate is that the cctv system can be easily tailored to the particular requirements of the premises being protected.

External cctv will rarely be found necessary in domestic premises, except for large country houses and the like. It will, however, prove very useful where there is a collection of buildings within a boundary fence – industrial complexes, market gardens, timber yards, etc. One of the major advantages of the cctv system is that it allows security personnel to investigate an alarm visually and from a position of safety. Without cctv a personal investigation would have to be made, resulting possibly in the security officer being attacked. This worry has often led to the security personnel ringing up the police before investigating an alarm, only to discover, when the police arrive, that the alarm was false.

It must, of course, be remembered that for a cctv system to be any good at all, its monitors should be under constant observation. It is possible, however, to incorporate a motion detector in the system which excites a warning buzzer and draws the attention of the guards to an abnormal condition. First vulnerable areas are defined on the monitor picture, then any movement within those areas will be sensed by the equipment and excite the alarm buzzer.

Cctv should not be considered as a DIY kit of parts, to be selected and stuck together without too much thought. The whole system needs to be selected and the individual parts chosen to satisfy the particular need. What is more, the equipment should be adequately maintained, thereby assuring many satisfactory years of service.

Natural lighting levels can be unreliable and this has to be countered by the

Fig. 11.12 Philips' Video 50 cctv camera

Fig. 11.13 Philips' Night Lynx camera

125

Fig. 11.14 Elbex (UK)'s Peeping Tom low light level camera

equipment to obtain the best possible picture on the monitor at all times. Illumination levels vary widely; from 100,000 lux in bright sunlight, to 100 lux at dusk, 0.3 lux in moonlight and 0.001 lux in starlight. In well-lit towns the reflected light from the sky will give an illumination around 0.1 lux.

Clearly, most cameras will work during normal daylight, but many will require floodlighting to operate during the hours of darkness. Even the highly sophisticated Philips Video 50 camera (Fig. 11.12) requires artificial lighting.

This camera is a good example of a cctv camera which allows considerable operator control and has many in-built devices to ensure good picture quality; for instance its on-board active processor which helps to produce high quality pictures in all normal light conditions throughout the life of the camera. Its body is environmentally sealed, which means that even in extreme conditions the Video 50 needs no additional protection. Also operational reliability is ensured because the camera is dust-tight and moisture-proof. Like other cameras of its type its functions, such as panning, tilting and zooming, can be remotely controlled. Furthermore, its automatic functions include:

- lens iris control which adjusts to light variations,
- gain control to maintain the best quality of picture at low light levels,
- dynamic beam control which gives better handling of highlights, and
- auto black which ensures better picture quality from varying scene quality.

But even with this type of sophisticated camera, floodlighting is necessary for the surveillance system to work at night. However, some manufacturers now have systems which work on exceedingly low levels of light. Philips' Night Lynx system, for instance, consists of a special camera and lens, together with a sophisticated image intensifier system, which works in all weather conditions from bright sunlight to the darkest night without floodlighting. The imaging system consists of a microchannel image intensifier and a Newvicon camera tube. In-built control circuits protect the intensifier from sudden high light levels, such as car headlamps. There is even a hand-held version of the Night Lynx camera (Fig. 11.13).

Cameras are becoming ever more sophisticated and compressed into an even smaller casing. A good example of this is the new low light Peeping Tom camera from Elbex (UK) which features a right angle 6 mm lens with auto iris and microphone, optional sync drive and preheater circuit – and all in a casing which can comfortably be held in the palm of one hand (Fig. 11.14).

Chapter 12

Special equipment

It has been the intention in this book to deal primarily with those aspects of security which are common to the general run of buildings, not to those with an abnormal risk factor, such as banks, building societies and embassies. These rather special buildings will clearly contain extremely specialised equipment – safes and vaults – which cannot be covered in a book of this nature, and indeed about which little is written, for very obvious reasons. However, as the level of risk seems to be rising in everyday buildings, hitherto uncommon equipment is starting to appear in what we have chosen to call 'normal buildings'. For this reason, this chapter has been included. It contains some basic information about a number of product types which are becoming more common in buildings today.

Information security

This is an area of rapidly increasing activity these days. Information has become a particularly prized commodity in certain sectors of commercial and governmental activity; and this has brought in its wake a quantity of special systems to ensure the confidentiality of information – whether it be personal data or scientific information. Most of these security systems depend on ensuring the security of computer systems and the information they contain. This is an extremely complex business and one which is undergoing change not merely on a day-by-day basis, but almost minute by minute.

Clearly this type of security is a subject in its own right and far beyond the scope of a general book such as this. The designer will anticipate that the space he provides for computer installations will contain a wealth of high-technology equipment and systems, many of which he only partially understands. To house these he needs a full briefing, undertaken by an expert in the subject.

There is, however, one more mundane aspect of information security that should be borne in mind – the privacy of the spoken word. This need have no sinister overtones. It can be simply a matter of allowing the manager of an office to discuss the salary of a subordinate without the rest of the personnel overhearing. This is a problem which has become markedly more difficult today due to the increasing use of open-plan office layouts or, where cellular office layouts are still employed, the low sound attenuation performance normal to most cheap, relocatable partitions.

There are two solutions to this problem. One is to design heavyweight partitions in those areas where confidential matters are likely to be discussed; the other is to fit equipment which emits 'white' sound to disturb speech intelligibility. The former is often impractical in today's highly mobile office layouts. Often the latter is the only viable course of action. White sound is a faint background hum which is not unpleasant or disturbing in itself, but which does make the overhearing of speech extremely difficult.

Mini-safes

For a relatively minor expense small floor or wall safes can be installed in many types of property for the storage of small valuable items, such as jewellery or cash. Applications can be as wide ranging as the private house, the private office or even the hotel bedroom (although a central night safe facility has more to commend it in most cases). One of the major advantages of these safes is their ability to be included in the original building with ease and be generally very unobtrusive – therefore often missing the attention of the thief. From this point of view the floor safe, hidden beneath loose floor coverings is a useful piece of domestic equipment. These small safes can also provide a degree of protection in the case of minor fires.

One example of this type of equipment is the Codebox safe box, developed in Norway and available in the UK through Codebox Marketing (Fig. 12.1). This

Fig. 12.1 Codebox safe boxes (Codebox Marketing)

129

seamless solid steel unit is easy to fit and comes complete with two wedge anchor bolts. Codebox safes can be fitted in groups or singly, each box being $120 \times 150 \times 250$ mm. They each have a single lift-out stainless steel plate door with no hinges or handles and fitted with an Abloy lock (see Chapter 5).

Pay windows

Because of the increasing danger of robbery where money is changing hands, security pay windows have become a common feature of offices (for the payout of petty cash and employee expense claims), ticket offices of all types, as well as the more obvious risk areas such as banks, post offices and building society offices. A few typical statistics of robbery are worth considering.

In 1982 there were 2560 reported armed robberies in England and Wales; 35% more than in the previous year. Offices, for instance, had experienced a 22% increase in armed robbery; theatres and places of public entertainment, 49%; garages and service stations, 40%; and banks, 116%. A typical example of the many types of security pay window, which are on the market at the moment, is the Type IV Pay Window from Chubb Installations (Fig. 12.2).

This has been designed and engineered to provide increased cashier security and clear customer communications. It is also easy to install in an external wall.

Fig. 12.2 Type IV Pay Window from Chubb Security Installations

Fig. 12.3 Type II Counter Screen from Chubb Security Installations

This pay window has a spring loaded steel transaction tray which, when opened by the cashier, allows a 25 mm gap only – sufficient for the exchange of cash, tickets, receipts, etc., but preventing hands or weapons passing through. The tray can be

131

easily locked in the 'up' position and also has a combined excluder/buffer strip on the bottom of the glass trim to prevent draughts. Two levels of cashier security can be provided depending on the type of glazing used; either 11.5 mm anti-bandit laminated glass for protection from hammer attack, or laminated spall limiting bullet-resistant security glass to give protection up to G2 and S levels (BS 5051).

Security screens

Security screens are mostly associated with high-risk buildings but are becoming increasingly used anywhere where substantial amounts of money change hands. Their design is varied and their levels of protection depend on the type of glazing material they contain (covered in some detail in Chapter 5) and the strength of the framework supporting the glazing (Fig. 12.3). One point is of considerable importance. It is of little use introducing a glazing material of high ballistic performance if the supporting framework does not have a similar resistance.

What is more, speech baffles or a microphone and speaker system must be fitted into anti-bandit or bullet-resistant installations to give audible transmission of speech from one side of the screen to the other.

Equally, doors in security screens must have a similar performance to the screen. An example of this is the Chubb Staff Security door (Fig. 12.4). This will withstand attacks by hand weapons (axe or hammer) and firearms up to G1 and S levels. By finishing the steel face on the attack side in sapele or black graining, the aesthetic appearance of the door is kept similar to the sapele veneer facing on the non-attack side. The doors can be fixed with overhead door closers to avoid them being inadvertently left ajar. They can also be used in pairs, each door being interlocked to control the traffic of personnel in and out of the security area.

The Chubb Staff Security door can be fitted with the Chubb CS2000 solenoid release and lock. This lock has three strong dead-locking bolts which are extended and withdrawn by the Chubb 3G110 lock (Fig. 12.5). When extended, the bolts engage in corresponding slots of the CS2000 electric solenoid striker box where they are held in position by a vertical sliding channel. A simple press-button unit activates the powerful solenoid, lifting the channel and allowing the door to open. When the door recloses, the striker plate automatically falls and locks again. Stainless steel casing to the striker box and a door edge protection plate strengthen the door against armed attack. In the event of a power failure, the door fails-safe in the locked position, although the unit can be opened by a key if necessary.

Entrance doors with a difference

In addition to such security entrances as turnstiles and gates, higher levels of security can be achieved by quite normal-looking revolving doors. Some of these can be remotely locked in any position, even when the door is running, effectively withstanding forces of up to 800 to 3200 Nm. One type of door – the Tourlock from

Fig. 12.4 Chubb staff security door

Boon of Edam, in the Netherlands (UK distributor, GHPA Contract Services of Harrogate) – locks by an electrically activated lock. If the power fails, the door would generally fail-safe in the free-running position, unless there is a specific request to the contrary.

133

Fig. 12.5 CS 2000 electric solenoid release and lock from Chubb Security Installations

There also are double door sets from this same company, called Swinglock doors. These allow one person at a time to enter or leave a security area, during which operation at least one locked door is blocking the opening all the time.

A device for passing parcels into or out of a security area without at any time leaving a clear opening is provided by another of this company's products. This is called the Packlock and consists of two cylinders, one inside the other, and with two openings in each. The inner cylinder has a central laminated glass divider and the whole cylinder can be turned through 180° by operating a push-button on the secure side. If anyone tries to force an entry by jumping aboard the device as it is turning, it can be instantly halted, imprisoning the intruder.

The latest in this company's range of security doors is the Circlelock which consists of two sliding curved doors within a cylindrical enclosure. One door is opened, allowing one person to enter the cylinder. This door then automatically closes and the exit door opens. If two people attempt to pass through the door together, a pressure mat in the floor of the cylinder signals the fact and the exit door will not open (Fig. 12.6).

Clearly most of this equipment is closely related to access controls and can be activated by the normal control means discussed in Chapter 6.

Medical alarm systems

In spite of their name, these systems can have a very specific security function in that they can be used to give alarm of any emergency which an elderly or infirm person might be undergoing.

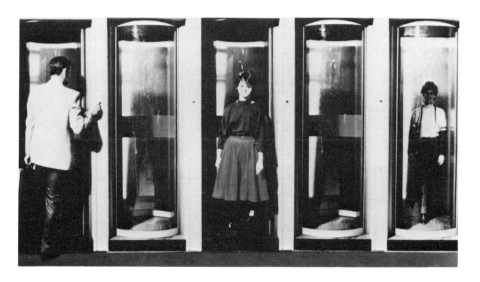

Fig. 12.6 Circlelock door from GHPA Contract Services

The Vitalcall system of Modern Alarms requires no hard wiring and is simple to install and maintain. The user wears a lightweight pendant radio transmitter which a simple pull on the pendant will activate. This call is received by a base unit which

Fig. 12.7 Firefly signs in light and dark conditions

b

automatically dials in sequence three previously selected telephone numbers of friends or relatives designated by the user. When a call is answered, the unit delivers a tape recorded message requesting assistance. At least two of the numbers have to respond for the system to be satisfied. Otherwise it will alert a constantly manned Vitalcall control station which will inform the relevant authorities.

In addition, the system incorporates a habit cycle feature which makes a daily check with the user to ensure that everything is satisfactory. In the event of no positive contact being made, the system assumes the worst and raises the alarm.

The equipment is self-diagnostic. The base unit reports in daily to a central computer which checks that everything is in full working order. During a power failure, there is a battery back-up.

Luminous signs

Although not a substitute for emergency lighting, the self-activating luminous material – Firefly – developed by Berger and its parent company Hoechst – can help to give vital direction indications when suddenly a building is plunged into darkness (Fig. 12.7).

Firefly absorbs light waves, whether natural or artificial, and emits them in the form of a bright glow when other light sources are removed. This glow will eventually dissipate after several hours, but it will help during those early minutes of a power failure. The pigment is totally safe, containing neither phosphorous chemicals nor radioactive material and it will continue to reactivate almost indefinitely.

A series of Firefly signs is available on semi-rigid self-adhesive PVC material, as well as self-adhesive strips which can be used to mark escape routes, or pick out hazards such as steps.

Chapter 13

Building site security

The building site offers the perfect setting for a vast array of minor (and some not so minor) crimes. Just consider the potentially lethal mixture of inducements, all of which we have met in different contexts earlier in this book, now all gathered together on the building site.

Firstly, location. Often the building site is, by its very nature, situated on virgin countryside or on unoccupied land in decaying inner city areas. It, therefore, is often not overlooked or policed by the general public; and, when the day's work is over, becomes undefensible space.

Secondly, accessibility. Once more, because of the nature of the work and the size of the area involved in large-scale building activity, coupled with the need to have free access at many points on the site, the area of operations is difficult to keep secure. The cost of erecting adequate security fencing around such a site, even only of sufficient quality to keep out the opportunist thief, is extremely high and is often an element that the builder will under-price in his tender and, as a result, spend as little as possible on when he comes to undertaking the work. If the specifier were more careful to detail precisely what type of security perimeter he required, there would be more likelihood that this element in the Bill of Quantities would be priced correctly by the tenderers. In addition, the specifiers would be able to insist upon an adequate perimeter enclosure from the successful tenderer.

Thirdly, occupation. During most of the hours of darkness the site will not be occupied, except possibly for the token presence of a nightwatchman or the occasional visit of a security patrol provided by a local security company. Neither defence is likely to deter the determined and professional thief, but may be adequate to combat the attentions of the local children.

Fourthly, stealable goods. The site is full of goods which are potentially valuable to a thief and ones which are readily disposable. As the price of building products rocket and the boom in DIY activity continues, an eager market can be found for almost anything which can be picked up on a building site.

Fifthly, vandalism. The building site offers endless amusement and adventure for young people. However good their original intentions, their fun will eventually lead to damage, both to the buildings being constructed and, maybe, to the vandals themselves. In this respect, the builder may well find himself liable for not protecting the site adequately if personal injury takes place.

Finally, we have already noted that certain classes of victim are seen as fair game by the petty thief. The employer comes within this category and so the building site becomes an extremely vulnerable place for what the shopkeeper would call 'shrinkage' – or otherwise refer to as staff pilfering.

Management solutions

Clearly, one of the most successful methods of dealing with the loss of materials and equipment on site is to institute a proper method of receiving and booking in goods on site, storing the goods (particularly the more easily disposable and valuable items) in secure compounds or storage buildings, and booking them out to individual operatives for specific work activities. This is a management function, not dissimilar to the stock control operations in most commerical and industrial organisations. It is, however, infinitely more difficult to carry out successfully on the average building site.

Site perimeter

The perimeter of the site should be protected, at least, by a fence which is sufficiently robust and sound that it will discourage the opportunist thief (see Chapter 11). Entrances onto the site should be controlled during all hours when operatives are on site. If necessary, intermittent checks of operatives' bags should be made as they leave the site. The knowledge that this might happen is usually sufficient to discourage pilfering.

It is obviously not possible to protect the site by a general intruder alarm system. However, notices that the site is under the protection of one of the security organisations will help to deter low-key over-night theft. The patrols of these organisations should pay visits at irregular, but frequent, intervals during the hours of darkness; and such visits should involve a patrol within the site, not merely a visit to the front gate and the offices.

Site lighting

As we have seen, lighting is one of the major deterrents to crime. Therefore it is advisable that at least the area of the site in which the storage compounds and store buildings are situated should have some adequate form of security lighting. It also would be a good idea to provide minimum lighting to the site offices during the night. There is often a quantity of valuable instruments in these buildings which might attract the thief.

Intruder alarms

As we have already mentioned, to cover the whole of the site with intruder alarm devices is usually impracticable; however, the site offices and the storage compound should definitely be protected. In Chapter 11 the use of outdoor detection systems was discussed. The storage compound can clearly be covered quite simply by infra-red or microwave active detectors, with their beams running inside and parallel to the compound enclosure. This method of protection becomes particularly economic when the compound is planned to be rectangular, or at least some regular shape.

The space between office and store buildings can be covered by criss-cross reflection of beams from infra-red detectors, using up to three mirrors between the projector and the receiver. This 'lacing' of the space between buildings makes it very difficult for the intruder to avoid the detector beam.

The offices, too, can be protected with a simple alarm system with door and window microswitches and pressure pads. Security stores may be fitted with vibration detectors which are triggered by the noise of the structure being attacked. Alternatively they can contain ultrasonic or microwave detectors to sense movement in the stores. Some proprietary security stores may even have an alarm system already installed.

Whatever the type of detectors and wherever they are situated, they should trigger off alarm bells or sirens and flashing lights – the more the noise and light, the better. This acts as a deterrent as much as an alarm to summon assistance. It must be remembered, too, that the site is possibly remote and the alarm bell or siren needs to be heard at a distance.

There are several stand-alone mobile intruder detector/alarm units on the market which, if placed in vulnerable positions, can prove useful on building sites. They are totally self-contained being battery powered and consisting of a normal form of intruder detector, an integral alarm and one or two flashing lights mounted on the top of the device.

Security stores

There are currently a number of proprietary mobile security stores on the market which can be used to house the most valuable loose materials on site. These are usually made of sheet steel, welded onto a steel frame. They have doors with high grade security locks, concealed hinges, overlapping surrounds which preclude the insertion of a jemmy, and reinforced surfaces around locking areas and at corners. The size range for such stores is vast, stretching from the small tool or flammable material vault, which are similar to oversized cabin trunks, to monsters up to 12 m long, 2.5 m wide and 3.25 m high, mounted on skids or jack legs (Fig. 13.1 and 13.2).

If there is cutting equipment on site, this must be stored in the most secure of places, as it can be used by the thief to gain access to high-security stores. Similarly, it should be borne in mind that if it is possible to operate any of the plant on the site,

Fig. 13.1 Large flammable liquid stores supplied by Safety Unlimited for the Ministry of Defence

Fig. 13.2 Steel site office/security building from Steel Building Systems

the removal of such items as tool vaults, or even larger security stores, in their entirety, to be broken into in relative peace and quiet somewhere away from the site, becomes a real possibility. Locking the jack-legs or fixing ground anchors protruding through the floor of the security store, are ways of deterring this type of theft.

Indeed, it is not unknown for large pieces of plant to be driven off the site overnight. Once more, this comes back to perimeter security. Whatever else is done in the cause of site security, one thing is paramount – it should not be possible to drive a lorry onto the site during the hours of darkness, load a lorry parked in a secluded rear area using the plant on site to lift the goods over the fence, and certainly not to drive diggers and other plant off the site. Finally, it is always wise to seek the advice of the local crime prevention officer and consult the insurers to make sure that the best levels of site security are established and being maintained.

Codes of practice and standards
Additional reading

The following is a list of references, some of which have been mentioned in the present text.

British Standards

3116:Part 4:1974 **Control and indicating equipment**

3621:1980 **Specification for thief resistant locks**

4737:Part 1:1978 **Requirements for systems with audible signalling only**

4737:Part 2:1977 **Requirements for systems with remote signalling**

5051:Part 2:1976 **Bullet-resistant glazing for interior use**

5266:Part 1:1975 **The emergency lighting of premises**

5445:Part 8:1984 **High temperature heat detectors**

5544:1978 **Specification for anti-bandit glazing (glazing resistant to manual attack)**

5839:Part 1:1980 **Fire detection and alarm systems in buildings: Code of practice for installation and servicing**

6206:1981 **Specification for impact performance requirements for flat safety glass and safety plastics for use in buildings**

6262:1982 **Code of practice for glazing for buildings**

BRE Digest

132 **Wilful damage on housing estates**

Industry Committee for Emergency Lighting Ltd

ICEL:1003:1982 **Emergency lighting applications guide**

Home Office Research Studies

34: **Crime as opportunity**; HMSO 1976

55: **Crime prevention and the police**; HMSO 1979

63: **Crime prevention publicity: an assessment:** HMSO 1980

74: **Residential burglary:** HMSO 1982

76: **The British crime survey:** HMSO 1983

Home Office Standing Committee on Crime Prevention: **Shoplifting and thefts by shop staff:** HMSO 1983

General Household Survey 1979/80: Central Statistical Office: HMSO 1983

Capel, Vivian; **Burglar alarm systems,** Newnes Technical Books, 1979

Design Council; **Designing against vandalism,** The Design Council, 1979

Doulton Glass Industries; **The safety glazing requirements of the new British Standard BS 6262,** Doulton Glass Industries

Jacobs, Jane; **The death and life of great American cities – the failure of town planning,** Jonathan Cape, 1962

Lighting Industry Federation; **The benefits of certification** – LIF factfinder 5

Newman, Oscar; **Defensible space,** Architectural Press, 1972

Advisory bodies

British Fire Protection Systems Association Ltd, 48a Eden Street, Kingston-upon-Thames, Surrey KT1 1ER

British Standards Institution, 2 Park Street, London W1A 2BS

Building Research Advisory Service, Building Research Station, Garston, Watford WD2 7JR

Fire Protection Association, Aldermary House, Queen Street, London EC4N 1TJ

Fire Research Station, BRE Borehamwood, Herts WD6 2BL

Glass and Glazing Federation, 6 Mount Row, London W1Y 6DY

Health & Safety Executive, St. Hugh's House, Stanley Precinct, Bootle, Merseyside

Industry Committee for Emergency Lighting Ltd, Swan House, 207 Balham High Road, London SW17 7BQ

Major companies in the UK security products business

Avoidance of Intrusion (Chapter 5)

Allen-Martin Electronics Ltd Marlborough Works, Thompson Avenue, Wolverhampton WV2 3NP

Bolton Gate Co. Ltd Turton Street, Bolton BL1 2SP

Chubb Alarms Ltd 42-50 Hersham Road, Walton-on-Thames, Surrey KT12 1RY

Chubb & Sons Lock and Safe Co. Ltd 51 Whitfield Street, London W1P 6AA

Chubb Security Installations Ltd Ronald Close, Kempston, Bedford MK42 7SH

Clarke Instruments Ltd 2 Dolphin Estate, Southampton Road, Salisbury, Wilts SP1 2NB

Colorado Electro-Optics Inc 2200 Central Avenue, Boulder, Colorado 80301, U.S.A.

Continental Shutters Ltd Maybank House Estate, Maybank Road, South Woodford, London E18 1ET

Garsec Ltd Bradford House, Bradford Street, Birmingham B5 6HG

Hakuto International (UK) Ltd Hakuto House, 159A Chase Side, Enfield, Middlesex EN2 0PW

Hazard Equipment Supply Co. Ltd Station Road, Westbury, Wilts

Kaba Locks Ltd P.O. Box 2, Tiverton, Devon EX16 5DS

J. Legge & Co. Ltd Moat Street, Willenhall, W. Midlands WV13 1TD

Locking Devices Ltd 309-313 West End Lane, London NW6 1RU

Medeco Security Locks Inc P.O. Box 1075, Salem, Va. 24153, U.S.A.

Minder Products Co 122 High Road, Leyton, London E15 2BX

Peak Technologies Ltd Warwick Road, Borehamwood, Herts WD6 1NA

Philips Business Systems Cromwell Road, Cambridge CB1 3HE

Racespace Ltd Anchor Road, Bristol BS1 5TT

J. E. Reynolds & Co. Ltd ERA Works, Short Heath, Willenhall, W. Midlands WV12 5RA

Scandinavian Aluminium Profiles AB Ltd Tibshelf, Derby DE5 5NQ

Yale Security Products Ltd Wood Street, Willenhall, W. Midlands WV13 1LA

Security Glazing (Chapter 5)

Alcan Safety Glass Co. Ltd Knowsthorpe Gate, Cross Green Industrial Estate, Leeds LS9 0NS

Chubb Security Installations Ltd Ronald Close, Kempston, Bedford MK42 7SH

Doulton Tempered Glass Ltd Ripley Road, Bradford

General Electric Plastics B.V. Sheet Europe P.O. Box 545, Wassenaarstraat 55, 4600 AM Bergen op Zoom, The Netherlands

Glaverbel (UK) Ltd Fraser House, 13-15 London Road, Twickenham, Middx TW1 3SX

Hat Glass Services Ltd 34-46 Newfoundland Street, Bristol BS2 9AX

Klingshield Klingshield House, 61 Chandos Road, Stratford, London E15 1TS

National Provincial Glass Co. Ltd Unit 26 Rotherhithe Industrial Estate, Rotherhithe New Road, London SE16

Northgate Solar Controls (Madico) P.O. Box 200, Barnet, Herts EN4 9EW

Renforth Ltd Lower Ardglen Estate, Evingar Road, Whitchurch, Hampshire

Access control (Chapter 6)

Access Control Systems Ltd 72 Winchester Road, Petersfield, Hants GU32 3PW

Borer Data Systems Ltd 6 Market Place, Wokingham, Berks RG11 1AL

Cardkey Systems Ltd 23 Stadium Way, Reading, Berks RG3 6ER

Chubb Alarms Ltd Hersham Road, Walton-on-Thames, Surrey KT12 1RY

Corkey Control Systems (UK) Ltd White Hart Road, Slough, Berks SL1 2SF

Erebus Ltd 377 Lichfield Road, Wednesfield, Wolverhampton WV11 3HD

Eureka Systems Dormey House, Upton Road, Slough SL1 2AD

Geemarc Trading Co. Ltd Lawford House, 1-3 Albert Place, London N3 1QB

GHPA Contract Services Ltd Dole Bank, Markington, Harrogate, N. Yorks HG3 3PJ

Hazard Equipment Supply Co. Ltd Station Road, Westbury, Wilts

Henderson Access Control Systems Ltd Kelvin Lane, Crawley, W. Sussex RH10 2ND

Peak Technologies Ltd Dayson Works, Warwick Road, Borehamwood, Herts WD6 1NA

Philips Business Systems Cromwell Road, Cambridge CB1 3HE

Tann-Synchronome Ltd Becks Mill, Westbury Leigh, Westbury, Wilts

Ticket Equipment Ltd Love Lane, Cirencester, Glos GL7 1YG

Yale Security Products Ltd Wood Street, Willenhall, W. Midlands WV13 1LP

Fire detection and alarm (Chapter 7)

AFA-Minerva Ltd Security House, Grosvenor Road, Twickenham TW1 4AB

BRK Electronics 12 The Paddock, Hambridge Road, Newbury, Berks RG14 5TQ

Chloride Standby Systems Ltd William Street, Southampton SO9 1XN

Gent Ltd Temple Road, Leicester LE5 4JF

Honeywell Control Systems Ltd Honeywell House, Charles Square, Bracknell, Berks RG12 1EB

MK Electric Ltd Shruberry Road, Edmonton, London N9 0PB

Photain Controls Ltd Unit 18, Hangar No. 3, The Aerodrome, Ford, Arundel, W. Sussex BN18 0BE

Racespace Ltd Anchor Road, Bristol BS1 5TT

S.E.S. Systems Southam Road, Banbury, Oxon OX16 7RX

Site Guard Ltd Guardian House, Thornford Road, London SE13 6SG

Tann-Synchronome Ltd Station Road, Westbury, Wilts BA13 3JT

Vikingshaw Products Ltd Osborne House, 12 Mount Ephraim Road, Tunbridge Wells, Kent TN1 1EE

Emergency lighting (Chapter 8)

Chloride Standby Systems Ltd William Street, Southampton SO9 1XN

Exem (Lighting) Ltd Cropmead Estate, Blacknell Lane, Crewkerne, Somerset TA18 7HG

Lab-Craft Ltd Church Road, Harold Wood, Romford, Essex RM3 0HT

Menvier (Electronic Engineers) Ltd Southam Road, Banbury, Oxon OX16 7RX

Saft (UK) Ltd Castle Works, Station Road, Hampton, Middx TW12 2BY

S.E.S. Systems Southam Road, Banbury, Oxon OX16 7RX

Pilferage and shoplifting control (Chapter 9)

Securitag (UK) Ltd 259 City Road, London EC1

Ticket Equipment Ltd Love Lane, Cirencester, Glos GL7 1YG

Volumatic Ltd Taurus House, Kingfield Road, Coventry CV6 5AS

Integrated security systems (Chapter 10)

AFA-Minerva Ltd Security House, Grosvenor Road, Twickenham TW1 4AB

Chubb Alarms Ltd Hersham Road, Walton-on-Thames, Surrey KT12 1RY

Cowie Fire Safety & Security Ltd Millfield House, Hylton Road, Sunderland SR4 7BA

Group 4 Total Security Ltd Farncombe House, Broadway, Worcs WR12 7LJ

Henderson Access Control Systems Ltd Kelvin Lane, Crawley, W. Sussex RH10 2ND

Modern Alarms Ltd 25-26 Hampstead High Street, Hampstead, London NW3 1QA

Pitts Security Gates Ltd Persec House, Kelvin Lane, Crawley, W. Sussex RH10 2ND

Security Centres Holdings Plc 113 Southwark Street, London SE1 0JF

Tann-Synchronome Ltd Station Road, Westbury, Wilts BA13 3JT

Vicon Industries (UK) Ltd Gunstore Road, Hilsea, Portsmouth, Hants PO3 5JP

External security and security lighting (Chapter 11)

AFA-Minerva Ltd Security House, Grosvenor Road, Twickenham TW1 4AB

Aro Dynamics Ltd Westmorland Road, London NW9 9RR

Wm. Bain & Co. (Fencing) Ltd Lochrin Works, Coatbridge

Elbex UK Ltd 49 Malden Way, New Malden, Surrey KT3 6EA

Frontier Gate Systems Ltd Tubeform Works, Cardigan Street, Birmingham B4 7RU

Group 4 Total Security Ltd Farncombe House, Broadway, Worcs WR12 7LJ

GTE Sylvania Ltd Otley Road, Charlestown, Shipley, W Yorks BD17 7SN

JAI Electro-Optical (UK) Ltd 1 Tavistock Industrial Estate, Ruscombe, Twyford, Berks RG10 9NJ

Man Barrier Corporation 32 Great Hill Road, Seymour, CT 06483, U.S.A.

Modern Alarms Ltd Security House, 259 City Road, London EC1V 1JE

Norbain Imaging Ltd Norbain House, Boulton Road, Reading, Berks RG2 0LT

Osram-GEC Ltd P.O. Box 17, East Lane, Wembley, Middx HA9 7PG

Peak Technologies Ltd Dayson Works, Warwick Road, Borehamwood, Herts WD6 1NA

Philips Business Systems Cromwell Road, Cambridge CB1 3HE

Pilkington Security Equipment Ltd Colomendy Industrial Estate, Rhyl Road, Denbigh, Clwyd LL16 5TA

Pitts Security Gates Ltd Persec House, Kelvin Lane, Crawley, W. Sussex RH10 2ND

Security Fencing Ltd 2 Church Street, Atherstone CV9 1HA

Tann-Synchronome Ltd Becks Mill, Westbury Leigh, Westbury, Wilts

Special equipment (Chapter 12)

Bristol Composite Materials Engineering Ltd Avonmouth Road, Avonmouth, Bristol BS11 9DU

Chubb Security Installations Ltd Ronald Close, Kempston, Bedford MK42 7SH

Codebox Marketing Ltd Indab House, 12 Lower Sutherland Street, Swinton, Manchester M27 3WE

Hazard Equipment Supply Co. Ltd Station Road, Westbury, Wilts

Stewart Fraser Ltd Henwood Industrial Estate, Ashford, Kent TN24 8DR

Building site security (Chapter 13)

Steel Building Systems Ltd Crown House, Armley Road, Leeds, W. Yorks LS12 2EJ

Index

Social and Community Planning Research, 26
sounder, 52, 72
specialist device, 4
speech privacy, 128, 129
standby lighting, 87
sub-master key system, 41, 57
surveillance, 22, 28, 103, 109, 124
sustained luminaire, 89

tag code, 68
tempered glass, 44
thief-resistant locks, 3, 35, 38
time recording, 108
tool vault, 143
toughened glass, 44
Tourlock, 132
turnstile, 119, 132

ultrasonic detector, 47, 49, 75

vandal temptation zone, 29, 30, 31
vandalism, 14, 25 *et seq.*, 139
vehicle detection loop, 119
vibration detector, 47, 48
victimless crime, 7, 8
visual alarm, 79
Vitalcall, 136
volumetric detector, 47, 48, 49, 121

ward, 34
warded lock, 34
watchman control monitor, 110
white sound, 129
window lock, 53
wired glass, 44